The Legacy
of the
Eagle and the Hawk

Tokya Chumash Cultural Arts
2771 Blanchard Rd.
Maricopa, CA 93252
U.S.A.
http://www.tokyachumashculturalarts.com
Tokyadave@aol.com

ISBN: 0-9713170-3-8

Printed in the United States of America
Cover artwork by John Schettler and David Paul Dominguez
Chumash line art by David Paul Dominguez
Photos by David Paul Dominguez

The Writing Shop Press
www.writingshop.ws

The Legacy
of the
Eagle and the Hawk

~ Chumash Legends and More ~

By

David Paul Dominguez

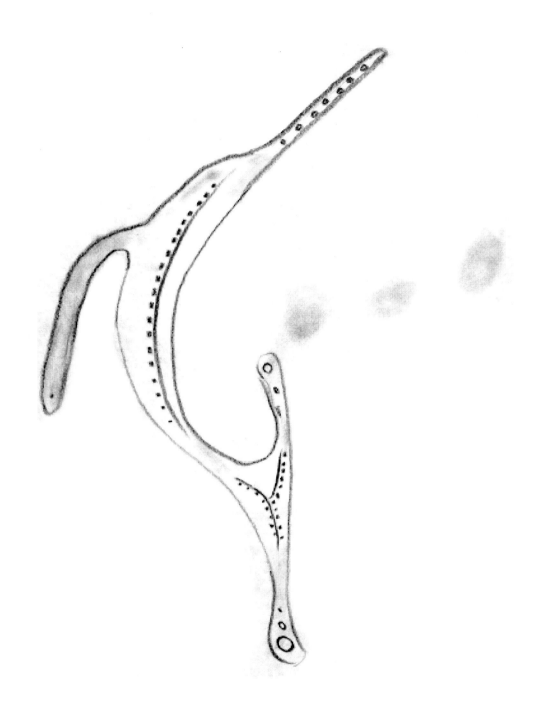

The Legacy of the Eagle and the Hawk

Props

These *Chumantics* are dedicated to my best friends and precious boys David, Daniel and Dennis Dominguez. My Mom, Pop and Choi Slow for showing me what integrity and family are all about. My Pow-Wow Highway ace/ duce brother and co-hort as well as my two gorgeous sisters. *Tani hey* for sharing that sibling love! To all the *Chumash* Peoples out there dedicating your lives to preserving our culture, tradition and pursuit of the *Chumash* dream: don't give up the fight! It's a long journey with many rewards and mysteries.

I would like to mention dearly, and with all due respect, that our tradition calls for us not to speak the names of those who have passed on to the spirit world. To one of our many Rez's spiritual leaders, *Tani Hey!* Yowa, Ol' Man, for being the pioneer and visionary in our *Molok* era. We *Chumash* Dancers, presenters, performers and story tellers, have you to be grateful for. Your beautiful dancing and regalia are still my inspiration today, as well as the many others that you have touched.

The scribing of this book is from the my experiences, imagination and *Mup Ta Yy* (my genetic memory) of my journey. My ideals, views and interpretations do not reflect nor represent the *Chumash* people as a whole and our varied ways of life and beliefs. Some of these legends are my interpretations of my greater grandmother's stories. I'm just having fun; nobody knows the truth but the Sky People.

This is for the love and joy of storytelling, and one of my ways of leaving a legacy. This is solely for my people, especially the *Chumash* youth.

I hope to convey a message to the *Chumash* youth, to learn and practice encouragement, vigilance, integrity, sincerity in your life to break the life cycles and movements that you have to deal with. You're not alone in your struggles. All of us have to struggle to be strong!

I wish to honor my love for our beautiful and creative, resourceful, igneous predecessors and my fascination and envy for their craftsmanship and ritual paraphernalia, as well as their ceremonial dance regalia.

I would like to mention our present day capabilities to be totally reliant on precious *Hutash,* (Mother Earth) and to diligently save her for our future families so they can have it like we do. She provides everything we need to exist and to envision destiny as far as peace and eternity goes. She's all we

have. Let's take care of her. We can't trade up.

The Sky People say that the universe goes on forever and there is plenty of room for everybody, there is no need to fight over it.

It is a mystery in the first place.

I hope all readers will find these writings a pleasure and a treasure, as well as what its true essence is really about, a message and a contribution.

So, what da' ya' say?

Ready?

Let's get ancient!

Hold on tight while I take us on a spin into the *vigilization* of the dream helpers that will transport you into another dimension.

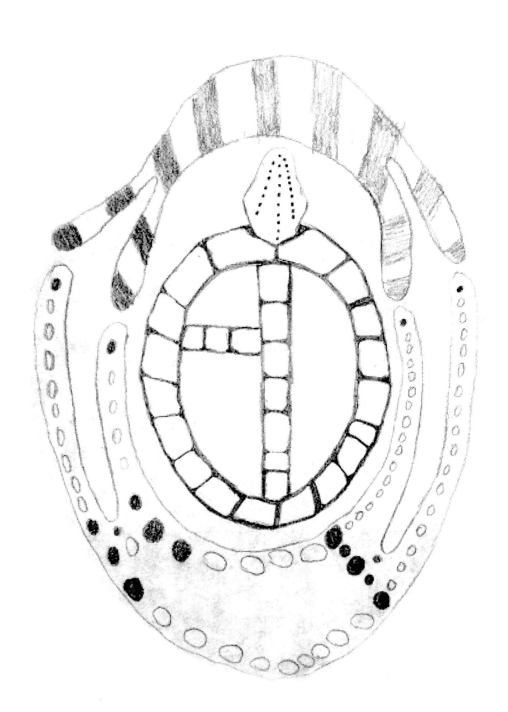

Timolokinash

When a *Chumash* legend, myth, folklore, fable, or story begins it traditionally starts with an introduction of a time frame when it reveals itself; when the animals were people, when the animals spoke, before or after the ice age, before or after the dinosaurs, before, during and after the rainbow. These are typical examples. I refer to these time frames as Molok eras; we capture a time frame in introducing our stories, prophecies, legends, and myths, an aura of essence and energy. Why? The reason has many answers depending on whom you ask. You ask a *Chumash* Elder or a modern day scholar who studies *Chumash* people and you are most likely to hear two totally different interpretations. I have my own interpretation and experience with some of these very old, sacred and powerfully real tales, and I am neither right nor wrong. However, I aspire to be a *Chumash* Elder some day, for I am Chumash. These movements take place on Mother Earth in the beautiful and bountiful lands of Southern California, in the Santa Ynez Valley, where resides the powerful River Turtle People from the village of *Kalawashaq*. The *Chumash* people believe the Sky People are gambling and playing a hand game with each individual, family and tribe.

These Sky People observe and are responsible for the spiritual movements and physical experiences that are encountered in the daily lives of traditional peoples. Sky People such as Sun, Moon, Morning Star, Sky Eagle and Sky Coyote are betting on which path an individual and family will follow. They wager depending on a person's use of knowledge, which has been acquired through a native belief system full of magic and mystery. There are strict adhesion to its rules pertaining to the use of plants, minerals and animals in their sacred preparations for rituals and ceremonies.

These wagers can consist of degrees of emotions, knowledge, chance, and other variables that empower an individual, family, clan or nation to navigate in the physical world. These legends reveal the past living lessons that were undertaken by our predecessors and orally translated for thousands of years to afford us foresight to navigate physically and spiritually when we come to find ourselves in one of these *Molok* eras. *Molok* eras have no time frame, nor box, that they have to fit in and conform to. They can last from one minute to millions of years, who knows?

I share these words of truth with respect for my predecessors' knowledge, way of life, adaptability, survival and reverence for their unique power.

I prefer to acknowledge the tribal families before us, as <u>predecessors</u>, the word <u>ancestors</u> assumes we *Chumash* people were extinct at one time. "We are part of a continuum!", as *Paha Pox* would say. "We are still alive and practicing." Tradition and culture are reflected in the discipline and the rigors of life, higher awareness and state of consciousness. These legends reveal some of the mysteries behind our powerful belief system and how they play in past, present and future generations of beautiful *Chumash* people. These legends are to keep the *Chumash* people in the light and out of the darkness that the invaders have tried to program us to believe. These are the good ol' days of *Chumash* prosperity, revitalization and freedom.

When the boats from the East approached the pure, lush shores of the *Chumash* Nation, their hulls were filled with beings obsessed with conquering, slavery and genocide. They were searching for the mystical land of Eden full of endless bounty.

They were victims of their own Karma, for they killed their own powerful prophet and their homeland was in shambles, full of disease and cursed with a dying environment that no longer gave life or sustenance. We beings of kindness and trust were easy prey for these people with an extensive background and history of ruthlessness and a reputation for ethnic cleansing. They could not grasp and live by the words of truth that were ministered to them and used as their shield to account for their acts of aggression, non-righteousness and invasion of one of the many North American Native Nations that past and present day scholars call the most advanced and wealthiest Nation on the West Coast.

After a few centuries we have found ourselves transplanted and assimilated, then dispersed back into our surrounding territories, our once powerful settlements and powerful places of mystery. We have not departed our dear Earth Mother, we are evolving and have summoned back our traditional ways, which are still alive within the magical sphere of the solar system and the relationship the Stars, Moon and Sun have with Mother Earth and her cleansing Winds along with the energies of Water, the power of the Rainbows, and the mystery behind the mighty Earthquakes of our region.

In these magical times that we find ourselves in, there are still a diligent few *Antap* practitioners who engage themselves in the mysterious movements of the *Sil' ee' uk.* Throughout the vast territory of Native America, we are known as Western Gate Keepers. In these technological and puritanical days, we are tapping the ancient wisdom and magic with our fortitude, discipline and dedication that are rare and required of the Sky People to be honored in the age-old rituals that keep us beings, in sync, balance and harmony with the rhythms of the universe, back in a natural flow, of our pre-

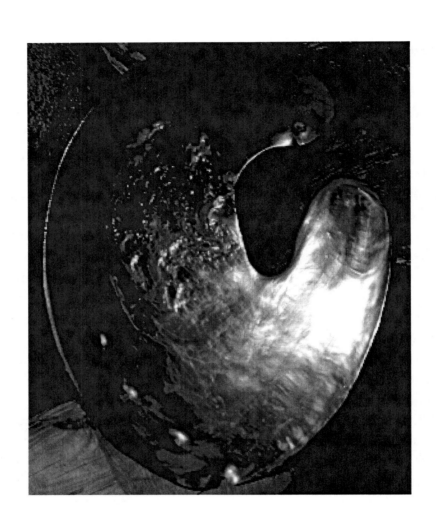

cious life giver!

The true life scenarios of this *Molok Era* are the time the Eagle and Hawk find themselves in.

The Eagle says, "It is a long journey", and he's right you know? No one says it's going to be easy, and it's not! His legacy of living and existing in a real time traditional way is unsurpassed and has a profound effect on many people, including myself, with his eclectic and hard core traditional ways. His philosophy, prophecies, commitment and determination has inspired my utmost love, respect and admiration for the Eagle *Wot.*

These are truly magical times that we live in *Paha*! Sure!

Choiy S'low, filled with ancient *Atishwun*, resides and rules the modern day Blackbird Clan, where the Powerful River Turtle People now call home. His captain *Heh' leh*, born of the Blackbird Clan to the Powerful River Turtle People, filled with the same magic has been gifted and honored to inform the coming generations of these times and a view of a legacy and alignment of modern day philosophers, seers, visionaries that are in the forefront of today's movement to keep our fires sacred and full of power.

Their validity does not rely on a "PHD." It goes beyond, beyond. Further than theory, assumptions and conclusions of a thesis and/or dissertation. Once in a while you can catch the Hawk babbling about:

What works for one person necessarily means that it will work for another. And is it actually working? And according to whom?

Living in real time and acceptance of what time we really are living in can be life altering, and changes a perspective of awareness and clarity in the way one chooses to carry their life and role in real time living. Just think if the whole world was on the same page?

But it's not! We are all individuals. Accept who you are and know your path. Have the courage to encounter any mystery that crosses it. The wisdom of knowing what to do, and more importantly, knowing what not to do, is essential! Integrity, character, magic, *Atishwun* is a gift that honors us by availing ourselves to the forces that exist, and encouraging a relationship through offerings and humbling one's self. Knowing that you are responsible for your own peace, and that this contributes to peace on a larger scale, is all important. It starts with your family, then your clan, band, then nation and so on till sky is the limit. Be secure in your own ways first and foremost.

Tani Hey!!!!
David Paul - Tokya, Chumash, Cultural Arts

Seeking the Autumn Wind

Forging deep into the Sespe Wilderness
the harvest moon has passed, sunlight lessens
and the road becomes desolate

In ritual dream time
I am screaming, confused, purged, comforted, sustained
by a Spirit Man who is weeping in both worlds

The fire embers glow
I see with my eyes closed
an inner spiritual vision

I discern, I affirm
life's ongoing journey of discovering the sacred in all
an enrichment of the soul

The more I seek, the more I find
As I forgive myself and others
I prepare the way for a new beginning

Releasing all thoughts, feelings and emotions that no longer serve me
I move past feelings of disappointment and betrayal

Always an opportunity to begin anew
I celebrate this experience of renewal
moving forward and upward with expectations and celebration

Spiritual discernment = wisdom of the soul
Apparent in dream time, the universe is full of alternatives
Clearly, I see the abundance of possibilities

The wind carries me home

Cuyamu
By Janet Janszen, October 2004 Nature Photography,
Poetry and Prose janetjans@earthlink.net

Part 1
Chumash Legends...

These are the Times

We Find Ourselves In!

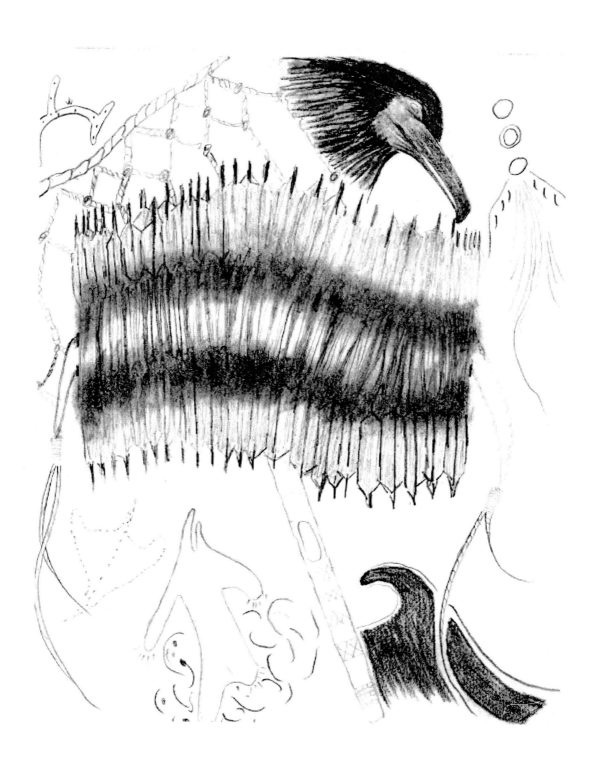

The Warrior

"The self-confidence of the warrior is not the self-confidence of the average man. The average man seeks certainty in the eyes of the onlooker and calls that self-confidence. The warrior seeks impeccability in his own eyes and calls that humbleness. The average man is hooked to his fellow men, while the warrior is hooked only to himself. Perhaps you are chasing rainbows. You're after the self-confidence of the average man, when you should be after the humbleness of a warrior. The difference between the two is remarkable. Self-confidence entails knowing something for sure; humbleness entails being impeccable in one's actions and feelings.

In this affair the only possible course that a warrior has is to act consistently and without reservations. You know enough of the warrior's way to act accordingly, but your old habits and routines stand in the way."

Carlos Castaneda
Quoting Don Juan, Yaqui Practioner

"A warrior is on permanent guard against the roughness of human behavior. A warrior is magical and ruthless, a maverick with the most refined taste and manners, whose worldly task is to sharpen, yet disguise, his cutting edges so that no one is able to suspect his ruthlessness."

Carlos Castaneda quoting Don Juan
Power of Silence

When a man embarks on the path of a warrior he becomes aware, in a gradual manner, that ordinary life has been forever left behind, that knowledge is indeed a frightening affair; that the means of the ordinary world are no longer a buffer for him; and that he must adopt a new way of life if he is going to survive. The first thing he ought to do, at that point, is to <u>want</u> to become a warrior. By that time knowledge becomes a frightening affair, the man also realizes that death is the irreplaceable partner that sits, next to him. Every bit of knowledge that becomes power has death as it's center force. Death lends the ultimate touch, and whatever is touched by death indeed becomes power.

The Legend of Paha Pox

This legend is what Paha Pox referred to by the remark, "These are magical times that we live in." *Paha Pox*, now he's one of them magical persons who live near the center of the world!

He has many mysteries and powerful spirit helpers. One of them is Coyote of the Seven Geese Boys who resides in the upper world with the Sky People. This is how the winds of *Soh'toh'nok'mu* share it with the Red Tail Hawk.

These are the times that we find ourselves in, whence this modern day tale starts as Coyote is out and about hunting and gathering in the *Samala* Valley, trying to fulfill the hunger pangs in his empty stomach. Whether it is a mouse, acorn, or stink-bug, Coyote will eat almost anything. On this day he comes upon a vulnerable Baby Raccoon crying inside a sage bush dehydrated and starving. "A perfect meal to start the day", thought Coyote. But first, a few questions from this tasty morsel. The Baby Raccoon got scared to death when that ferocious canine spoke to him. His first instinct was to run but he couldn't move. He was so panicked that he just begged Coyote not to eat him nor trick him either, because he was taught by his parents that Coyote will always try to trick you to eat you. But for some reason Coyote did something that was very un Coyote of him. He assured the Raccoon that he would not eat him nor trick him and promised to honor it. And Coyote was sincere because he was coming from his heart and not his stomach.

He asked the frightened tike where his parents were? The Baby Raccoon replied, "he and his parents were chased by a Mountain Lion and were separated." Coyote, tried to convince Baby Raccoon to trust him and to come with him and let him help the Baby Raccoon. That day Coyote gathered and hunted while Baby Raccoon rested in Coyote's house. He prepared and cooked a delicious meal of bulbs, crawfish and all kinds of tasty new foods that he had gathered and watched as Baby Raccoon devoured and relished the new cuisine. As time went on, the two arch rivals embarked on a relationship unheard of in this *Molok Era*.

They found themselves living as one and being, part of a unique balance. Coyote, taught the Baby Raccoon to gather bulbs, seeds, and nuts.

Most of all, he taught him to hunt in the streams with his arms the way raccoons feel for tasty Crawfish. Coyote, even showed him a plant and taught him how to prepare it to soothe his aching belly when he had eaten too many of them scrumptious, fat Crawfish.

One day, after a few seasons had passed, Raccoon, full grown, was headed to his favorite gathering hole in the river in a mood that he was truly enjoying. It was one of them days when every thing seems to just fall into place. What a life! Crystal clear vision; he was very aware of all the movements in the universe as he stumbled across a feisty Baby Bobcat that was in an attack position, poised and ready to leap at him from a low branch.

At first, he was startled, then acted like he didn't see him. Because of the deep state of consciousness he was in, he was able to get really close to the furry lil' cute kitty that, after an awkward silence, he couldn't help from snickering it seemed so hilarious. Raccoon couldn't stop from laughing out loud, he had tears streaming down his face he laughed so hard. Just made the lil' guy even more spunkier and feisty and he wanted him even more. After Raccoon had his fun, he calmed him down and shared his story of how he was orphaned when young and was helped and taught how to live, hunt and fend for himself by a Coyote that he still lives with.

Baby Bobcat listened and agreed to trust this delicious, fat Raccoon. He agreed to meet this unique Coyote. But he still couldn't believe it. He was nervous, giggling and curious. A Coyote? Naw! So, the two headed for some food, rest, and sanctuary. At first Coyote was nervous with an orphaned Bobcat in his house. Especially one that kept staring at Raccoon like he was dinner. But the little guy kept his manners, so he was allowed to stay on.

Coyote always had an admiration for the way the Bobcat people lived. He wouldn't have to raise him by himself either, Raccoon was a full-grown juvenile now and could hold his own in this world. The two orphans seemed to get along, just like siblings. So Coyote found himself sharing his dwelling, knowledge, and living skills with a Baby Bobcat as well as a young Raccoon.

As time went on somebody found an orphaned Baby Bear Cub, then an orphaned Baby Skunk, then a Baby Jackrabbit, then a Baby Fox, then a Baby Badger. Next thing you know Coyote had Seven Orphan Boys sharing his dwelling and with time and with all the combined gathering and hunting skills, not to mention the variety of foods he was eating. Coyote didn't need to gather or hunt anymore. He had plenty of time to pursue the many activities that used to occupy his time before his path changed from bachelor to being a father, uncle, cousin and mentor. One of his passions was working and weaving plant fibers into ropes, nets, and some very mysterious magical cords. With these magical cords he wove Eagle-down into them.

Coyote, had this irresistible, fascination with flying and he recalled an Elder of his had shared with him, "if he could find out the mystery to the feather-down-cord he would be able to fly." So Coyote's fascination turned into passion as he spent the majority of his time dancing, singing, and weaving and working the magical properties of this wonderfully fibrous plant with soft feather down.

One day he was singing to *Alisha Kakanupmawa* (sun) and, when he was finished, Grandfather showed his gratitude by telling him to wrap the down-cord around his head and think with all his might that he would get off the ground. As he started to wrap the cord around his head he started to levitate and float off the ground! Pretty soon he was able to jump at extraordinary heights and distances. Then one day he just took off like a Bat out of *He'lo* and started to fly! At first he was able to stay in the air for a few minutes then he was flying from the mountains to the coast, then to the Islands and back. He mastered flying at high speeds and unbelievable heights. He truly mastered what he sought after so vigilantly. He was having so much fun! So now, more than often, he was taking off to other territories where the Seven Orphan Boys couldn't find him.

Then one day, Coyote took off on one of dem' long journeys, once too many times. It was enough to get the Seven Orphan Boys stirred up and curious about the Elders coming and goings. They counseled amongst each other and devised a plan to spy on Coyote and find out what the Elder was up too. So the Orphans used all their skills and knowledge and spread into the territory. They had to keep their movements a secret, they knew Coyote, they knew he knew, they knew. It was quite a predicament. Ha! Ha! Coyote, was a keen stalker and knew how to work his camouflage. But most of all, they knew he had a magic stone that he could use to see.

He was a very talented seer and they didn't want to rouse his suspicion. Pretty soon one of them came across a place that looked liked the Elder was frequenting, and they were all Mooptafied by the strange tracks that he was leaving. They would just seem to end. Like Coyote, they just disappeared and vanished into the winds.

At first all kinds of ideas entered their thoughts, then, all at once, they had this mysterious feeling hit them. At the same time they all looked up to witness Coyote diving right at them! They all ducked and ran for cover, cause it seemed like this Elder couldn't master the controls that were driving him. But he had it under control and was just showing off and having fun. Boy, were they ever stunned, silent and *Mooptafied!* They yelled and yelled for him to come down but it seemed to them that the Elder didn't hear them. "What a sensation these bird peoples had going on," he thought to himself, as he kept on flying towards his first destination, for he was already in a trance-like state. So they decided to wait for him and, after a few weeks passed, they got tired and went back to their fires. What they didn't know was that Coyote had just got up into the air when they came upon his take-off power spot.

And Coyote had plans! Big plans! He had made a lot of nets and ropes for bartering and trading. He was planning on bartering for an Eagle bone pan-flute that was inlaid with precious beads and had a beautiful harmony that was made by a Bear at Cuyamu. He was gonna stop at the Islands and trade Pelican for a black soapstone arrow straightener. Boy, did Coyote have really big plans! And Coyote always went outa' his way to catch a good hand game at *Quasil* or *Stuk*. He even had plans of checkin' out the beach scene at *Humaliwo* and the maidens at *Upop*.

When he arrived back home, the Orphans couldn't be found and their fires looked like they didn't come back from their encounter. Oh well, they'll get tired of waiting and start back soon, he thought to himself. So he just rested up and ate all the food that was left behind by the Orphans. He knew they were going to be so excited and full of many questions. Especially the one how a "being" without feathers could fly? They were relentless in the pursuit of asking him every waking moment and then some. Because they all had grown into responsible, well mannered young men, he felt they had earned it. So he started to teach them very slowly and did a lot of laughing. He told them that there was only one rule, and that was they couldn't go past the clouds. They could fly around in them but you are not supposed to go beyond them. Why, they asked? He said that he really didn't know. All he knew was that the Elder told him so and that should suffice.

So they all started to learn the magical properties of the Pox fiber cord as well as the Geese down that Coyote had honored them with. We all know how Coyote loves fat geese! He had been saving the down for years and took just a long time to master flying. They accomplished jumping, at first by tying the cords around their heads, but, they couldn't fly. However, they were the best jumpers in the territory for years and it was rumored that Jackrabbit could jump to the Islands and back!

One day one of them had the idea of tying onto each other and, as the last one was tying on, they started to levitate. That was the mystery for them! They had to be like a flock of Geese. Seven being as one! It was very clumsy at first, cause of them being tied, but after a few moments they were flying in alignment and even in a big V Geese pattern to climb high with the air currents. They got higher and higher, and all at the same time they thought of what the insides of a cloud might look like and ascended towards the first one they saw. It was beautiful and breath taking! They were mesmerized by the beauty and feeling.

They felt like real Geese. It seemed to them that they were just a little faster in the clouds, a little more graceful and acrobatic. One of the Orphans was so memorized by the beauty, that he veered too high and dragged the rest of them with him. Do you know that he turned into a Goose right in away? And, as the rest followed, an easy feeling crept over them as they themselves turned into Geese! Now they really could fly faster and higher than they ever had before. All the time this was happening Coyote was watching and was flying towards them.

But they were way too high! Still, he had a tremendous heart now, that was the trade off when he gave up hunting. So he followed and a warm feeling enveloped him as he turned into an Eagle. As they were absorbed into the world of the Sky People, they started to change again.

This time they were brightening up and starting to glow into stars. So tonight when you give into the magic of the Sky People and give the Moonlit sky some attention look at the Big Dipper very carefully, those are the Seven Geese Boys! Pay special attention to the second star on the end of the handle. It has its own Moon! That Moon Star is Coyote, Paha Pox! What magical times we find ourselves in.

Ya Hey!

The American West And The Burden Of Belief

The oral tradition of the American Indian is highly developed realization of language. In certain ways it is superior to the written tradition. In the oral tradition words are sacred; they are intrinsically powerful and beautiful. By means of words, by the exertion of language upon the unknown, the best of the possible — and indeed the seemingly impossible — is accomplished. Nothing exists beyond the influence of words. Words are the names of Creation. To give one's word is to give oneself, wholly, to place a name, than which nothing is more sacred, in the balance. One stands for his word; his word stands for him. The oral tradition demands the greatest clarity of speech and hearing, the whole strength of memory, and an absolute faith in the efficacy of language. Every word spoken, every word heard, is the utterance of prayer.

WESTWARD HO,
N. SCOTT MOMADAY

Baby Eagle

"Timolokinash" When the Gopher and the Bear with green eyes.

In the territory at the center of the *Chumash* universe, it snows during the winter and is scorching hot at the height of summer. It is a very powerful place to live, and only the hardiest of beings can exist there. Two of them are the majestic bird families of the Golden Eagles and Condors. Now we know there's this thing called opposites attract, right? Well, this is a legend that conforms to that philosophy. You see, there was a dashing Condor that was courting and wooing a very vibrant, caring, beautiful Eagle. A storybook romance, just like in the fairy tales. Who'd ever think that an Eagle and a Condor could fall in love, take the sacred vows of marriage and ride it out thru the thickest of the thick and the thinnest of the thin? It is one of them Chumantics that rivals the love Coyote has for Duck and her beautiful ways and gracefulness. Hopefully, one of these days someone will ask that darn Coyote what that is all about? So, as the story goes, Condor approached and presented Eagle's father with a multitude of gifts, with all sincerity, and asked for his approval to marry his daughter along with a promise to care for her the rest of their lives together.

So that is how it all started! And this is a doozy! That resourceful Condor built a dwelling on a high cliff overlooking majestic mountains with beautiful valleys with an abundance and assortment of game to hunt. Do you know that Eagle loved the dapper Condor so much that she would not allow him to go out scavenging any longer, whereas he would stink up the house so "bad" that it would take her all day just to keep it clean, fresh, and all the maggots and flies away? As we all know, Eagle is a great hunter and she was honored to do the hunting and the preparing of the their food. Besides, she was a woman, and we know how women are about their shopping and traveling from store to store. However, more important it was also a way for her to get away and have time for her to meditate and observe the movements of the day, for she was very deep and intense. Just like an Eagle!

Boy, did she ever spoil that dashing Condor! He was eating fresh, fat, plump game 24/7. She brought home fat rabbits, squirrels, and plenty of his favorite Canadian geese when in season. Did you know that dashing Condor even started to smell good and grow a Bear belly? Then, suddenly, the mighty movement of the Moon brought about an egg and a new baby hatchling adding to the families growth. Both were overjoyed and anxiously awaiting the arrival of their new baby. And we all know how parents are when the preference of the child is concerned. The father yearned for it to be a boy, and the spitting image of himself. And moms? Well, we all know they would favor a little girl to help with the chores and do those girlie things together. Well, this little fortunate first born was a baby Eagle boy. And was father Condor in a happy state of confusion! He was deliriously happy and a very proud parent of a baby boy, however, the little offspring looked dead off like his mother. In this world all positives have a negative and all the spoiling and inactivity that the father Condor was experiencing sort of went to his ego and head, and he was losing control of his heart. So, as the baby Eagle started to grow into a handsome young fledgling, the father's love for him turned into jealousy and envy. It wasn't the father's fault either, because he didn't know any better himself, for he was now losing ground within his heart.

Boy, did that ever confuse the baby Eagle? This was his father that he loved and cherished and looked up to for guidance and support. He was just a fledgling and was so confused by the behavior of his dad, so he continued to take the abuse and felt sorry for himself. Then the winter spirit blew in like a ton of bricks. Yikes, was it rough, cold and blustery in them high mountains! This baby Eagle had no other choice but to toughen up and live it out. As this winter was as tough as any to blow through, towards the latter part of the grueling season the game got rather slim and mother Eagle could barely keep all three of them fed. On top of that, she was gone most of the day, so there was no neutralizer or referee in the nest. That didn't help father Condor's mood. He wasn't like Mr. Bear, who lived off his belly, he needed food and was not a happy camper as he was used to being treated like a king by the mother Eagle. So he treated the baby Eagle even worse. It came to a point that the baby Eagle had had enough and flew away from home. What triggered it was this: every time Baby Eagle tried to snuggle up to the warm smoke hole at the top of the dwelling, the father Condor would continuously knock him off from the inside or toss sticks and stones from the outside. It wasn't fair and after one of those confusing, abusive days, Baby Eagle took flight. His mom tried to find him, to no avail, so she tried to and talk some sense into the father Condor, imploring him to search himself.

But father Condor just stayed home and ate while the baby Eagle spent most of his time in a pine tree along a river hidden deep in the forest. He was so depressed that he didn't have the enthusiasm to hunt, nor did he have the urge to even eat. So he just stayed in his newfound spot and sang and cried his heart out. Unbeknown, below him on the trail, was this certain

Coyote whom was on a journey which took him right by Baby Eagle's big pine tree, and all the singing and crying got his attention. It made such an impression on his heart that he felt sorry for him and compelled to help as well. However, he was in a hurry, for he was on his way to visit a cousin who had adopted a baby Raccoon and needed some assistance and help. Who new that this valuable lesson would come in handy to help his cousin, because he was Coyote and all he could think about was that his cousin had a fat, scrumptious Raccoon in his possession. Just the thought of that made his stomach growl and his mouth salivate.

So a few weeks went by and, on his way back from his journey, he was surprised to see that that darn baby Eagle was still in the tree sniveling, singing and feeling sorry for himself. So he pondered a solution to the co-nundrum that revealed itself in front of him. He knew that the spirits had something in mind for him because he learned a few things from his cousin and the gift of the heart of helping others. So out of the blue, this baby Eagle hears a voice coming from the river trail down below. It was a Coyote, and the Coyote was asking if he was okay and if there was anything that he could do to help him? Not a Coyote! Mother had warned him that those Coyotes were tricky and were always trying to take advantage of a free meal. So he asked what the sly canine wanted and was surprised, curiously, as all the Coyote wanted was to say, Baby Eagle sounded better singing than cry-ing and had a beautiful voice that shouldn't be wasted by crying and feeling sorry for himself. And that was enough to get baby Eagle's attention, for he had longed for attention and someone to talk to. So he flew down to a low enough branch, to listen to what this Coyote had to say, and at the same time cautiously stay out of the reach of those fast paws and tricky move-ments.

Coyote was wily enough to engage him quickly into conversation to trick this young Eagle into revealing why he was crying, and, before you know it, that darn baby Eagle had spilled his guts out! What a relief to him it was! So Coyote worked his magic again and quickly lured the baby Eagle into listening to his story about a cousin of his who adopted an orphaned Raccoon. He also got firm with him, and scolded him, and told him to straighten up and act like the Eagle that he was.

Coyote convinced the baby Eagle that the situation would work out a little better for all concerned if he contributed to the balance of the family by hunting, for it would surely take the load of his mom's shoulders and she would be able to spend more time with his father and his father wouldn't have idle time to pick on him. Boy, did the baby Eagle like that idea! So he looked into his heart and would take the advice of Coyote and put trust in the spirits to help him in this trying dilemma. By golly, was that Coyote ever tricky in a knowledgeable way! He had the young Eagle captivated for hours, and he reminded him that he was very lucky to have both parents alive and reminded him about the orphaned Raccoon. So, to all you kids out there that are reading this story when you are having problems with your parents: take a lesson from that tricky Coyote and the problems will work themselves out. If you have any doubts, pray to whom you ever pray, and let them take care of it. Do you know that the baby Eagle is a very good friend with the Seven Orphan Boys? Whoop, Whoop!

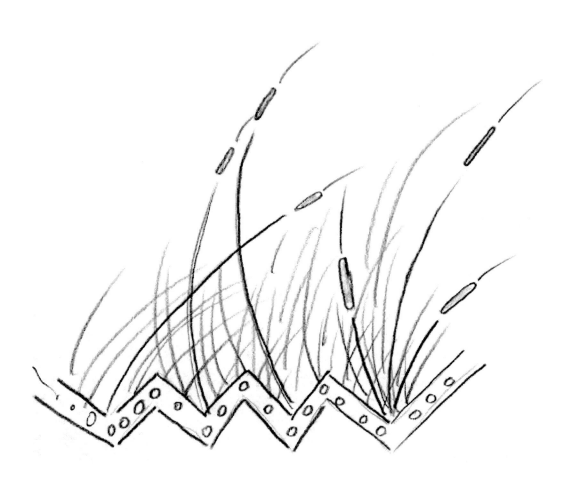

The Crow and the Mockingbird

"Timolokinash" - When the Birds Sing

Did you know that the Crow and Mockingbird were siblings at one time? And, unbelievably, they got along just fine and didn't fight and hassle each other as they do now? In fact, they hardly ever, fought. True fact…Until they hit puberty and their hormones kicked in. What a time! Remember Boyz? Remember the warm fuzzies the cute girl down the street gave you? Or the girlie next door sneaking glances at you in class? Get the picture? This girlie was all that and a bag of acorns. You bet! A bag of acorns! She had cascading blue velvet hair and intriguing, inviting aqua colored eyes, which drive all of us Crazy Birds, well, Crazy Birds.

One look, from those mesmerizing peepers and she hypnotized them into her charming, coquettish ways. She had them vying for her attention like two, love struck teenagers. They were shadowing her every move. They followed her so much it reminds you of the Vulture peoples circling a carcass left by Mountain Lion. She had them acting very silly! Then something peculiar happened, boys will be boys and Crow got brave, broke the ice, and kidnapped Bluebird from her perch to stash her away in a cave where Mockingbird could not find her. Sort of like in the old days when women were a shortage and/or if a buck found a female in another Clan he devised a plan and took her away. I guess taking what one wants was the way to go back then. Makes one ponder where the cave men stories come from?

Any who, another peculiar moment arose and Mockingbird found out where she was hidden and took her from the Crow while he was down at the oak savannah chomping on them fat sweet, delicious acorns. Those acorns will get you every time! Well Mockingbird had the advantage, didn't he? He knew the ways of his now ex-sibling and new nemesis, arch rival. So, when it came time to figure out Crow and where he would hide her? Who better else than Mockingbird to find that adorable, charming Bluebird. So he waited a few days for Crow to settle so he could figure out how to confuse and outwit his new opponent he knew, that Crow travels East, towards the rising Sun in the morning, and flies West in the evening and can be spotted at the same time at his various pit stops during the day. That was Crow's power but also his downfall, he was so predictable you can pretty much know the time of day just by his whereabouts. So, the plan Mockingbird devised consisted of timing; timing is everything, and you can pretty much set your watch by Crow. While away on one of his jaunts, Mocking bird flew in and snatched that breathtaking Bluebird, right out of the Crow's nest.

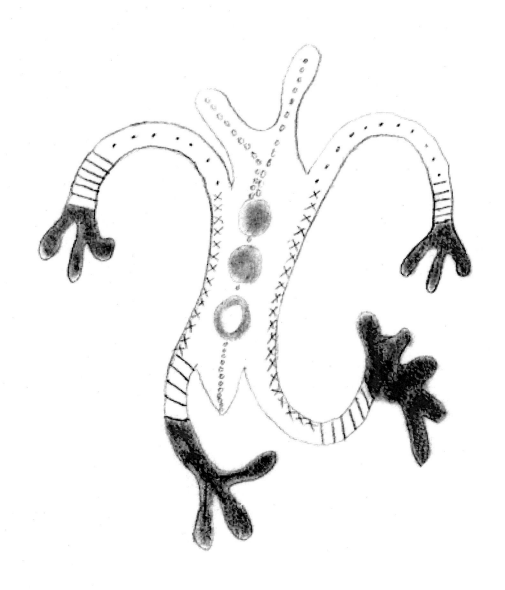

The Legacy of the Eagle and the Hawk
Qaqs' Dream

"Timolokinash" During the change over from Spring to Summer.

This is a present day storybook romance whose dynamics revolve around the mystery of love, a physical attraction and genuine caring that started as beautiful as the sunrise, and ended as quickly as the sunset lacking its beauty.

Qaq, the Raven is well known as a powerful dreamer, singer and dancer. During his days in Cuyamu with Slow the mysterious, powerful dark colored Eagle, he had plenty of time to delve deep into those powers and apply them to finding a mate. What a fusion of fun and reality. He achieved amazing success due to the use of his Moop ta my and Atishwunits ways. He was just a tad heartless and cold blooded when it came to love. Either, his Karma was playing on him or he had been hurt by love, one to many times. However, his heart did a full 180, when he was rescued from the storm of life, and found himself living with the Eagle. What an honor to be instructed and tutored in the fine art of tapping the powers and mysteries of the universe through various expressions and rituals. They quickly developed a relationship unheard of in those days and were attaining amazing feats of magic and prophecy.

Who would think a fortunate, powerful person as Raven, would be lonely and in need of companionship? It's true! Ol' boy was lonely and a hopeless romantic. Even though he was handsome, lithe and very personable, he found himself practicing singing and dreaming in a life companion. He knew about being careful for what you ask for, because when you get it, you have no control over the dynamics nor the outcome. Love sorta' has a way of disguising those traps and the Sky People had some lesson to teach him about the nature and characteristics of love and it's interaction within himself.

Can you guess what is part of the mystery here? I'll help you just a lil' bit. The spirits gifted him with a song that he called his, "Indian Girl song". And he sang this song during his power times to conjure up a beautiful, fun and wealthy woman to share his life with. While he was preparing to attend and dance at a social circle in Yokuts territory, he had one of them dreams that he immediately recognized to be a prophecy and was to be carefully deciphered and approached with the utmost caution. He knew that dreams are generally classified into two categories. Ones that are of the sub-conscience variety and then there are the dreams that are profound and contribute to the destiny of your life. Those he takes seriously.

While in this dimension Qag found himself flying over a river and spotted an inviting branch perching over the center of the fast flowing, mesmerizing aqua current. He had been in search of a meal all day and was facing a lil' adversity while being tested for his resourcefulness and durability to gather and endure the approaching days that were growing longer. As he was gathering his composure and quenching his thirst to ease his empty belly, he watched as Onso the Steel head trout was gathering and congregating in it's deep cool depths. He was intrigued and spellbound as he noticed their tails and fins where acquiring the luminous hues of the rainbow. Their tails and fins were growing longer, brilliant and more radiant as he studied the subtle and gentle movements flowing with the dance of the pristine current. As more and more of the beautiful fish gathered beneath him he was surprised that he could see into the water as if he had fish vision himself. He was amazed and intrigued by the appearance of a crystal house that started to form right in front of his very eyes.

This was no illusion and was crystal clear as the house and dream itself. Curiosity swept over him as he noticed that a beautiful woman was beckoning him from within this magical shining dwelling. He forgot all about the hunger of his stomach as the emptiness of his heart took control and he found himself instantly in love without knowing anything about this maiden whose hypnotizing eyes lured him instantly into her mysterious grasp. He was star-struck and enthralled by her beauty, that in no time, he found himself fumbling with his words of introduction.

She soothed him with her sensual voice and regal demeanor as he was asked to take a seat next to her fire of kelp, sea grass and drift wood. She easily took control of the conversation for he was tongue tied for what seemed like an eternity, he was confounded when she answered that her name was Luhui. And that she was! A true Island princess. Just as beautiful as the name that purred from her luscious lips. He was instantly mesmerized and curious about the enthralling beauty that was seated in front of him! He couldn't believe what just had transpired right before his very life?.

However, there is one twist, that is not widely known, and hopefully and probably it will stay that way. While she told him her adventures and kept him captivated in a tranquil glow a cinnamon colored Fox with a silver stripe down his back jumped out of the fire, swam around them with the brilliantly colored swimming fin beings, turned to Qaq and said, "I'm the Steel head trout of the land and Onso is the Fox of the fresh water world. "Correct" Raven thought to himself? Just like the Dolphin is the Coyote of the Sea, and the Condor is the Swordfish. And with that started the world wind romance between the Princess and the Raven!

What magical revealing times these are? Wouldn't you agree? So, while you are pondering and absorbing this, remember! Be careful for what you sing, dance, and dream for? As for the story to the ending? You'll just have to ask the Raven if he ever got over that beautiful Island Princess?

Sutiwayan ul atuc!

How the Stones Went From Soft To Hard

Who would have known , as hard as stones are today, they used to be soft? They were just as loved, admirable and fascinating with lots to say and share, just like today? They were! That's how Daniel heard it in school. No joshin'! It's an honor to know that our children are hearing and seeing the Chumash culture in our schools. I'm not the only one, sharing our ways and stories. *Tani Hey*, thank you for touching my sons spirit and the many of other kids that you are effecting with the sharing of this story and our beautiful culture and traditions.

Now, these Elders the stones, as they are known by in Native Circles, are the eldest beings here. They are just parts of *Hutash* that have loosened up and separated due to the shifting of the plates that are constantly moving that we live on. Back then most of the four legged flyers used them as gathering places as well as their enjoyment such as sun bathing, picnics, they would even build fires on them to keep warm and cook their meals.

They would cook all kinds of different dishes. Meals of the seeds and bulbs, fresh game such as rabbit, quail and deer. Fish from the ocean along with various shellfish. And the stones loved it! Those beings knew exactly where to locate a suitable and soothing fire site. The stones really loved the aroma of the atmosphere and would actually miss it when the beings were not around.

As for the four legged and flyers, who wouldn't love jumping and tromping on these large and soft trampolines? They would have contests to see how high one could bounce and tricks that would outdo each other. They used to team up in three's and these contests would last for days at a time. However, some of the time they left the stones bruised and sore. And the stones really didn't complain either. Sorta' nice getting the attention. Everybody loves attention. Nobody is exempt from this. We are so used of living in large families, even now that affects us. However, that is for another time.

This went on for thousand of years until three beings sorta' spoiled it for everyone by getting carried away and not knowing when to stop, even after the pleas of the stones. This trio comprised of *Cheechio* the Bear, whom had a very long tail at the time; *Chiquiti* the Barn owl, whose *mug* was just as sleek as the Hawk and the Eagle; and the Western fence lizard *Onok'ok*, whose belly was a light grey and brown at that time. The way it went, this huge stone that was frequently visited by the clan called a council among the rest of the stones and came up with a remedy without any serious repercussions to either side. So it was voted on to ask *Hutash* to make them a lil' harder so the beings could still gather, yet not leave em so sore from the jumping. She agreed and replied that it was a balanced conclusion, however, she said that they couldn't turn back and that was the downfall. They accepted and that's how they turned hard. But that's not the end of the story! There is still the matter of the trio, they are the ones that started this whole confusion and mess. Their first attempt to have fun after the stones turned hard was a day that would effect the three for the rest of their lives.

The first incident of that ill- fated day started with *Chichio*, the bear who loved to bump on his rump and jump on his pogo stick like tail and scraped his tail right off as *Chiquiti* the owl scraped his face and bent his nose, while *Ononok'ok* got a big surprise when he hit the hardened stone, not to mention a blue belly from a belly flop. True story.

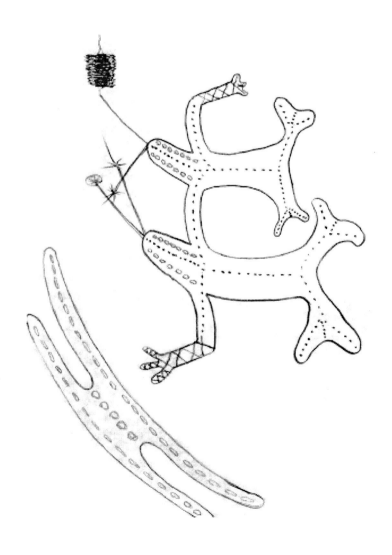

Life Courtship

Life is one long courtship of things we want or fear.

Whether it is something, we want, or something to avoid. We court it, we woo it through our thoughts and words, reaching with intense effort. When our desires are too rigid, we have been known to create a psychological wall that shuts off the natural flow to carry out our heart's desire. We simply can't do what we want to do. When something is to be avoided at all costs, we tend to vision it so vividly that it has no choice but to come our way. The same mental law turns back what we want as well. We have to be careful about what we want, because we are apt to get it. It is our nature to court, but wisdom should always be there.

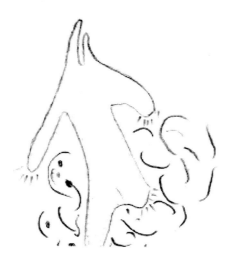

January First

If, like a Cherokee warrior, I can look at the new year as an opportunity to stand on new ground, then strength and courage are on my side. If I have waited a long time for everything to be perfect, and there have been moments, brief as they were, that filled my expectations, then I can face the challenges. I will remember that things *do* work out. Bodies *do* heal, relationships mend, not because I said it, but because I believe it. But it is time to make things right, to stay on the path. As water runs fresh and free from the woodland spring, so new life and meaning will bubble up.

Joyce Sequiche Hifler

The Little Girl Of The Lake

This is a lesson for all about families and cherishing the families we have and the families we are born into. This is a legend about such a family, they consist of a young girl, her mother, family bond, and values.

People search the world over for phenomenal works of mother nature and her intriguing shapes and designs of terrain. The interaction of the flora and fauna is so intricate that it cannot help but manifest power. Us *Chumash* have been gifted with many examples, and this is about one of them, that will be around for a quite a few generations to come. It's a water filled, dormant volcano, shaped into a powerful medicine circle that is home to many beings of different characters and physical attributes. And for thousands of years we have been tapping the secrets and interacting with the mystical villagers that inhabit the womb of this unique water circle with no bottom. One of our traditions is going to the shores and presenting offerings of food, textiles and shell bead money with prayers to these people and the lake spirits.

So one might wonder why these people were chosen, or choose, to live away from society and the norms to reach the epitome of higher living? It is not as easy to answer as it might sound. However, we know there are a few of us in this present day world, who would do anything for higher enlightenment or for the opposite—fame, fortune or easing the loneliness of not loving one's self.

You see, this little girl and her mom lost their father and husband early on in life and left them alone early to fend for themselves. There are many powerful and large bears in this territory and one of them took this hunter's breath from him in a life battle over a deer slain by the beloved warrior and provider. As time went on, the mother and daughter consoled and kept each other company and followed tradition by taking their offerings and prayers to the lake every morning. This went on for many years and, as the little girl grew older, she sometimes took on the task herself when her mom was out gathering and preparing food for them. If ever there was a widower who deserved a man in her life to help her it was this woman, she was doing the work of two and was grateful she had just one daughter. She toiled very hard every day to keep them both fed and content as well as clothed in the best of skins the hunters had to offer. She made very beautiful baskets of deer grass and pine needles that she traded and bartered with to buy whatever they needed to survive.

After years of toiling these baskets were well sought after and prized by the women of the territory. So with that she carried much prestige and grew rich with shell bead money. Then one day like a bat outa' *He'lo*, that man that she so much deserved and conjured up, came into her life and swept her off her feet like the great tide medicine of the ocean. The mother's attention now had to be split with sincerity between the new beau and her young daughter. As time went on the boyfriend had most of the attention and the daughter was being increasingly ignored. The mother wasn't in the heart and soon forgot how hard she and the daughter had it and soon grew lazy and spoiled.

Soon she always seemed to be in a bad mood. Not like the way she used to be, very jubilant and rambunctious. It got worse as time went by and the mother became even meaner and took the daughter for granted. She would yell and scold her for the dumbest and ridiculous things. The mother got to a point that she told the lil' one that she was grown up enough to make the offerings by herself and to leave her and her new husband alone. Because this little girl was very young and was solely raised by her possessive mom she didn't have many friends, so she would just stay at the lake and *vigilize* at the edge and cry while she yearned for someone to talk to and put it out there for the spirits to hear. One morning, after she was told to take the offerings to the lake, she was crying and crying when she heard a little girl voice just like hers. It sounded like the voice was asking, "Why are you crying so much?" She looked all around her but could not detect a sole insight, then she paid attention to the water, and a girl about her age came out of the pool asked her not to cry. At first she was terrified and nervous at the presence of this little girl whom suddenly appeared out of the lake. The water girl, consoled and reassure her that it was okay and not to worry and be scared, she had been watching and listening to her cry and plea for some days now and knew how she felt and wanted to help. She asked if she wanted to have some fun and go swimming in the lake instead of being unhappy and crying? The young girl replied, "no", that she was warned and told not go swimming in the lake, it was considered taboo by all the villagers. Her new friend said that they would not see her because she would be invisible. Invisible? She couldn't believe her ears! Invisible? Boy, that would be fun! "No one would miss me", she thought to herself. So she agreed.

While Sun was approaching his crystal house in the Western Gate of Mystery, and the two new friends were embarking on a bond for life all lost in new fondness, the mother was worrying on the whereabouts and tardiness of her daughter and went to the lake to investigate the doings and had thoughts to scold her.

You see, the mother was in her mind and not in her heart and the mother was going to send her home. To her surprise and avail, all she could find, was a couple sets of footprints that seemed to be going in and out of the lake. She yelled and screamed for her daughter over and no one seemed to respond but, *Pu lu ee* perched in one of the oaks absorbing the peacefulness and the time of sunset. She dared not go into the sacred water. She was so petrified she didn't know what to do? So she ran to the *Wot*, and he informed her that he couldn't help. However, he gave her some advice to seek out an *Alchucklash* whom had *Alalkoy* and the *Onso* as his dream helpers.

The unique combination of salt and fresh water swimmers gives one an advantage when it comes to swimming the depths of the lake. The Elder said that there was one of these doctors known to live around *Quasil*, and to take him all the bead money she had.

Upon finding this certain *Alchucklash*, he listened intently while deciphering what was needed to aid this terrified lady. He said first, that his service was always paid for such valuable advice, second, she would need all her weavings as gifts and offerings, third, she had to undergo purification first thing when she got home. She was to be prepared by first light to meet him at her daughter's footprints by herself, no exceptions. Early the next morning she anxiously waited and wondered where the *Alchucklash* was? He suddenly popped out of the water, grabbed the baskets, and told her to be back in three mornings, and he added that she should not talk to anyone about it and everything would be fine. He then vanished back into the depths of the mysteriously powerful, cold, water circle. He had to dive real deep and be within his heart to find the opening to the air pocket that led to an underground world occupied by beings with one foot in the physical world and one within the spirit world. He asked the whereabouts of the girl. He was relieved that the mother saved a lot of her baskets, many questions that required an offering. Finally, he was successful in his navigation and walked right upon her, and her friend, frolicking as if they knew each other for a lifetime.

He tried to persuade her to accompany him back home, and informed her that she had two days to come up with an answer or a solution. He said her mother very much missed her and paid much money and possessions to get her back. However, she refused to go. Finally, on the last evening, it was decided that she needed at least go back and tell her mom that she was going to stay because she was truly happy, and to hug and kiss her one last time to ease her worrying. She knew that the mother would understand, for she was now in the heart and not in her mind.

Do you know that the mother went on to live a long prosperous happy life? Yep! And that little girl is still swimming in that sacred medicine circle, sharing her mystery with others.

Did you know the Chumash culture is alive
and thriving on the California Coast?
Ritual events and ceremonial dance festivals
are held regularly. Contact the author for
booking information!

Teshna the Humming Bird

Why is the subject of ego always popping up? My guess is "ego" is the most likely culprit that will humble you the most with "fate." This is a tale about that conundrum, and three grand birds and their quest to the tap the powers of the Sun.

Back in the days, Humming Bird was just as large as Condor and Eagle. They were the largest three birds around and they were the best of friends, until fate most likely had its dirty little paws in it. And one must assume, by now, who fate is and what he looks like. Does he have candy stripes and purple polka dots on a teeny, weenie, bikini? Who knows? Well one secret is that Humming Bird is a girlie and Condor and Eagle are boys. No kidding! Talk about competition and spitting contests. It was always do best or die for that ill fated Humming Bird, for we all know how small she is.

It's no big secret.

Right?

Or is it?

Well, this is the secret of how she got so teeny weeny and colorful. You all know how much power Sun has and all the rumors of successful bounties obtained precede him. Well that intrigued the Humming Bird. She was especially tempted, curiously, about the tattle being told of the powers, obtainable by venturing so close to him, you could grasp the power right into your wings. Anything you wanted! And that haunted her every thought, so she devised a plan to get there, and not alone!

She invited fate!

You bet!

Fate!

And fate was disguised as Condor and Eagle. You see, they knew her like the back of their wings.

Since Humming Bird was just a little bit larger, sleeker and faster, she won a majority of the competitions. When she was young, she was taught to be very humble about it and be a good sportsman by her Mother, Grandmother and the rest of the Humming Bird Elders. As she grew older and more independent, she slowly forgot the way she was taught and not to mess with the men of the Condor and Eagle families. Then fate showed its ugly paws again. She really thought that she could fool Condor and Eagle into a journey to the Sun with just taunting her prowess over Condor and Eagle, hoping to damage or insult their pride. You know how proud Condors and Eagles can be, especially, the thing about being males! So they wanted to make it interesting and, in turn, play on Humming Bird's pride or, as "fate" has it, "ego." So she agreed to the terms of it not being a competition and that they would all take equal amounts of food and water. And fate turned into a journey to the Sun.

They were adamant about all starting out at daybreak the next day and keeping a steady pace. Reinforcing, that it was not a competition! They all started out together on an even, steady pace, a little faster than the Crow flies! Well, as Condor tells it, when it got closer to mid–day you could hear Sky Lizard making a bet with the Sun that he couldn't draw in the fate of the Humming Bird. Then Condor explained that the Moon wanted some of the action. After all, Humming Bird is a girl and not to mention, *her* girl! So Morning star backed it up and fate turned into a gambling game. Everybody knew that Humming Bird's "ego" would get the best of her and was mere fun for the Sun, except the Moon! Her faith and magic is unsurpassed and it gives her husband, Sun, a little competition of her own.

So, during that power time of the mid-day Sun, Humming Bird found herself in the grasp of Sun's magic, and was caught in an unbreakable spell that had her flapping those big wings of hers faster and faster as she got closer and closer to the power of the mid-day sun. As Condor and Eagle yelled to get her attention, and tried to keep up, Grandmother Moon used her water magic and splashed a little on the speeding Humming Bird.

Humming Bird was flying so fast that when the water hit her it scorched her like the colors of the rainbow. Did it work, you might ask? You betcha! She started to regain her senses and had to flap them big ol' wings faster and faster, and then she noticed every time the Sun pulled her back into his grasp she would shrink, little by little, and she was already small enough to disappear. She tried even harder to regain her momentum , even if that meant that she had to flap her shrinking wings a gazillion times as fast to escape the death grip of the Sun and his daughters. Finally, like a slingshot, she shot out of his grip like a Bat out of Hello. Oh yeah, I forgot to mention that she is so embarrassed about her exploits that she cannot stop blushing. Dem Girlies?

The Rainbow Bridge

After the ice age and the big melt down, the great salt water world started to reside and you could count, on one hand, the few small pieces of *Hutash* sticking out of this turquoise and aqua colored landscape. One of them, large peaks we call the island of *Limuw*, is also the island the *Sky People* selected and gave life to the *Chumash* and where *Maquiticock* the spotted woodpecker planted the first acorn. The first *Chumash* lived here for thousands of years in peace, beauty and harmony.

These first people were people of vision and were curious to know the mysteries and bounties of the large land mass across the ocean from them. For many generations it was envisioned and attempted by the strongest of warriors to swim across the great salt water. For many families it was pondered if their brave family men would make it across or would wash ashore like the many who have tried before them. A very old powerful *Alchucklash* of that era was perplexed and intrigued about the conundrum that was such a challenge for much of his life time and until now he had avoided its mysterious grasp. He had watched as it brought on a frenzy amongst the men, by just the mere mention of the thought.

So he approached it very much like the rest of them, with sincerity. He contemplated and prayed for an answer through purification and fasting. Then, one night during a very intense moment, *Evening Star* spoke to him and said he would assist in searching for an answer in dream land. You see, one thing about this certain *Alchucklash* was that he possessed a powerful charm that connected him to the beyond, and the powers of the *Sky People*. The first night of his dream, *Sky Condor* created a large *Mishtoyo* spanning the ocean to the mysterious shores of the great land mass. The second night in his dream world, *Sky Lizard* showed him and his people crossing the colorful *Mishtoyo* and being greeted by all the beings that had gathered on its shore. Then, on the third night, he dreamed of *Sky Eagle* instructing him and his people to look ahead and cross the *Mishtoyo* with determination and they will make it to the other side.

So he gathered the leaders of the families and recanted his three dreams and they, in turn, gathered the people. They all patiently waited for the sign of a circular halo around *Sky Grandmother Moy Moy*, which was to indicate the start of the journey at day break the following day. Three nights later it appeared in a cosmic radiance that extruded an essence and aura of purity and clarity. The next morning as *Kakanupmawa* used his torch to caress *Hutash* and all her children, these people of vision who believed in the message of the *Sky People* embarked on their journey across the colorful vapor that was suddenly appearing in front of them. As they were half way through the energy field, a few of them started to change, and they found themselves slipping, little by little, through the colorful feeling fog.

It was like a flash fire. One individual went from his heart to his mind and lost confidence, and it spread like a wild fire. One thing we know about the nature of man is that he is very skeptical. The *Sky People* are fully aware of man's skepticism and foresaw this and conferred and agreed to an antidote if such a crisis arose. As they lost total confidence in the message, they fell through and headed for the waiting depths of the great salty.

The *Alchucklash* pleaded to the *Sky People* for a solution and he heard *Sky Eagle's* loud voice roar for the people to stay determined and look ahead and that it would be as envisioned and they would reach the approaching shoreline He watched from the shores with the other beings as his relatives hit the water and turned into the first *Alalkoy*. The old timers say there used to be a rock on *Limuw* that bore the same resemblance of *Mishtoyo* and had beautiful paintings that were dreamed by this certain *Alchucklash*. So these are the times we find ourselves in, heh?

Celebrating Spring With the White Deer People

Some of us Chumash people anticipate the arrival of the Spring Spirit and the message, alignment and relationship of fertility and the White Deer Person, whom in the past few years arrived in our territory. The event of spring is a continuum of and age-old earth changeover experienced by all us people as we walk on two or four legs, swim or fly, grow leaves, fur, hair, scales or feathers. Some of us are coming out of hibernation and shedding our winter coats. For some of us we are starting our grand migration journeys and mating rituals. Others are starting the evolution from bud to flower. Some are just venturing out spiritually. We all greet and welcome the spring spirit with great anticipation of ritual observances. I myself feel like a spring Chicken Hawk, waking the Bear spirit out of hibernation and of being one with the long nights and short days winter has to share. We renew our commitments and obligations to the nurturing of our families and their legacies. We welcome new children into our societies and acquire new roles and obligations as well as responsibilities. Grandfather Sun and Grandmother Mom are starting their journey into longer days and shorter nights, with the gambling gaining more intensity as it is being played amongst the Sky People.

Us poor pity-full two-legs also celebrate with our movements and rituals of song and dance. Our offerings and sacrifices represent commitments to our roles in our belief system and our use and respect for Mother Earth and her natural resources that provide everything we need to survive. In the spring we renew our obligations to welcoming new people into our sacred circles. This spring we acquire a new obligations to understand the representation of fertility with the arrival of the White Deer person living amongst us. The timing and balance of that person contributes to our health and balance. We want to insure its fertility and legacy by staying together as a people in a harmonious and respectful way, honoring each other's visions, prophecies, dance and song.

We have come a long way as a people and sometimes we need take a time out and honor our achievements and prestige. Time has a way with how nations grow and nurture themselves, and each other. Remember every morning that the Sun rises out of the east that we are born again. East represents the dawn as well as the Spring time. Remember that ol' saying, "Everything is Sacred." Funny how time is? We as a Nation must be doing something right? We have two White Deer Persons, now.

These are the times we find ourselves in!

The Silence of the Heart

Everybody is lonely or needs love, and
attention. It is just a matter of how high you
set your morals for yourself. How you hold
yourself and what you are willing to give up of
yourself. Most of all, it is what you are willing
to hold onto.

Heh Leh
Winter 2003

Part II

Those Darn Coyotes . . .

Dem Darn Hoo Haws

"Timolokinash" When the Coyotes Share A Story.

This here is what you can compare to an American joke. It is also not meant for the ears of the lil tikes. Sorry! But it's a dirty joke. The White Deer fell in the mud! Ha! Ha! Ha!

There were these two Coyotes gazing on the overlook above the settlement of *Kalawashaq*. When one of them mentioned that the villagers referred to him as Magical Coyote Dancer because he is the most Magical Coyote Dancer their eyes ever have beheld at their celebrations. The Coyote sitting next to him took a double take and was astounded at the remark his comrade had just uttered, for he was under the impression that his name is Magical Coyote Dancer. He inquired of his companion how he came to the conclusion of this quagmire and suggested a solution to the present conundrum. Now, remember now? We are dealing with Coyote, fast witted and quick as a whip with solutions and remedies. Remember the Road Runner cartoon and how Coyote is always figuring a way to catch Road Runner using gigots and gadgets, do dads, thingamajigs, what-ya-ma-call-its, do hickeys and gizmos as well as zoom zooms and wham whams? Well, this one suggested that they should make it a game of challenge and chance, for Coyotes are great gamblers and he proposed that they each take turns running through the village to see what name the locals would announce them as. As soon as he had stopped speaking, the other Coyote took off like Bat out of Helo, down the hill running at full speed using his charm stone that could make him as fast and sure footed as Mr. Antelope. With such a fast running start the Coyote left behind in the dust could only catch up in time enough to hear the villagers yell that it was, Magical Coyote Dancer! As the delayed Coyote approached the village and shouted, "another one approaches!" So that is how, Another One, received his name. Whoop! Whoop!

There was this one Coyote who's attention at the moment was occupied with the pond he was approaching to elevate the cotton mouth and to quench the thirst he was experiencing due to extreme heat the of the Summer Spirit and the long day he went without. He was startled and caught off guard as Ol' Mr. Cooper Hawk flushed out of a tall Pine tree and roosted on another farther down the valley. He was even more surprised and astonished as all the bird peoples came out of hiding and high tailed it the other way! They were all hiding and still as mousses in houses as they all came out of the

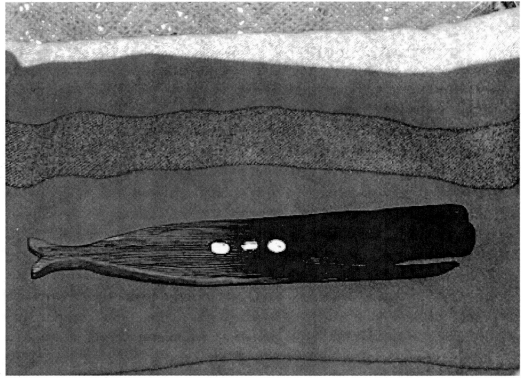

Native artwork takes many forms, with magical creatures fashioned
from paint, charcoal, wood and shell.

woodworks! Ol Mr. Cooper Hawk loves to eat medium and small sized birdies and is known to visit their gathering places. Flicker flew one way, Blue Jay followed as well as Red Wing Blackbird and Spotted Woodpecker. They were everywhere, small ones and large alike. The rush was on to loose that Ol Mr. Cooper Hawk. A sight to behold! Guess you had to be there!

Bet ya didn't know that Coyote is a poet and didn't know it? Surely, I might be joshing and jesting ya as a colorful recantor would surely go about it, or, there is a fraction of a possibility, I might be pulling your leg? Not a chance! Give this a whirl Earl!

Shssh!
You got to be very quiet at night!
Da Bears!
Da Bears come out at night!
Dat's Right, Da Bears.
Da Bears come out at night.
I'd be scared of da Bears, at night!
How bout you?
Would you be scared of da Bears?
At night?
But, da Rabbit not scared of da Bear.
How come the Rabbit not scared da Bear?
I would be scared da Bear if I was da Rabbit?
At night!
How bout you? Would you be scared da Bear?
At night?
I'd be, scared, da Bear! At night!
But he not scared!
How come da Rabbit not scared da bear?
Cause he got a Magic Nose.
Dat's right! A Magic Nose!
Da Rabbit got a Magic Nose!
He twitches it and he turns Indivisible.
Dat's right, he turns Indivisible!
However, if you had a Magic Nose?
Wouldn't you have big claws like da, Bear?
I would!
Wouldn't you?
Wouldn't you have big teeth like da Bear.

Dennis Dominguez showing his painting skills!

And be just as large and as powerful as da Bear.
I would!
How bout you?
Would you be big like da Bear?
So who knows?
Maybe da Rabbit is da Bear?

And what did Squirrel do to have to go thru life annoying every person that he encounters or crosses his path?

I remember a time of pondering and being taken into daydreaming and wonderment of what it must have been to live in the days when the beings where just like us. They spoke to each other and had the same senses and characteristics that effects our every day of lives? No kidding? Would I try to pull the wool over your eyes as Coyote dressed up in sheep's clothing? Or can this be one of them subjects up for discussion that should be saved for another place and time?

Have you ever contemplated what the animals looked like when they spoke to each other and were just like us human tribal peoples? Some of us *Chumash* traditional peoples feel they change appearances and acquire new powers when *Hutash* cleanses herself. We figure that she has done it twice, the eras of the dinosaurs and the ice age can be viewed as two of these movements, according to the studies of mankind. We know that these types of movements happen in threes, which is also the sacred number to the *Chumash* people. However, we'll discuss that at another appropriate time. What's up with Time?

This is an insight how Bat changed from a beautiful sparrow, with a reputation as the best archer in the territories, to the person we all know today. So we'll call him Bat as well, and watch him shift. Back in the old days, Sparrow and Coyote were allies when it came time to go to war at the request of the Wot. They were his favorite duo to call upon when there was time of conflict and he needed the services of these powerful warriors to defend the integrity of the village and the families to go to battle for them. How they fight is mighty intriguing and a sight to behold. Sparrow clings to Coyotes back and shoots arrows while Coyote sneaks up and positions himself for their advantage and at the same time he is fast enough to dodges arrows and get in a few shots himself.

How they came up with this strategy is another mystery to be revealed at another time. They are a very respected and feared twosome when it comes to the awareness of tribal war. This time frame takes place when they were

Author and Pow Wow dancing at Coarsgold for Lupe Dancing Bear.

very active and were in search of spirit and dream helpers. Coyote and Sparrow were overlooking a large settlement early one day and were enthralled and amazed at its large terrace, and the alignment of the houses in the settlement, then their thoughts became one in their meditation. Both were meditating on the movements of the purification the men were undergoing at the Men's Lodge. Then the mighty wind spirits blew in and revealed to them that it was their time for them to learn the purification rituals of the Men's Lodge. So they gathered all their shell money to present to the Paha of the village for permission and advice on building the Men's Lodge.

His tutelage lasted many days and when they were finished they watched the *Sky People* as instructed for an alignment that would be the proper time to build it according to the *Paha's* teachings. They built a subterranean style lodge on the side of a nearby river ledge with the door facing the water so they could cleanse themselves with the water spirits after the purification of the fire. The *Apyoke* was made of thick sturdy willow poles and a mixture of tule reeds, sea grass and adobe. It was a very impressive purification dwelling for their first attempt. *Paha* was very explicit and detailed about the building and the movements the spirits required.

The next morning Sparrow was up before Sun poked his torch over the eastern gate and was gathering wood and stacking it by the entrance to the newly built structure. He waited for Coyote for some time till he concluded that Coyote was sleeping in, and it was no surprise to him for that was part of Coyotes ways! So he went inside and started to build the purification fire. When Coyote awakened, he had totally forgotten about the purification that morning and made himself a big fat delicious goose for breakfast, with all the fixings. While he was eating, he suddenly remembered his obligation to Sparrow and rushed to the lodge like a Bat outa' *He'llo.*

He figured by the location of grandfather he was running a little tardy and hoped that Sparrow wasn't angry and would be sympathetic towards him. Then he saw the smoke and he knew right away that he was running late and that there was a possibility that Sparrow might be very angry. But his comrade, Bat, wasn't the least concerned, and very understanding, because he was in his heart. So he entered while Sparrow closed the door behind them and started to add more wood.

As they proceeded, he asked Coyote if the fire was too hot for him and when Coyote replied no, Sparrow added some more wood. They sang many songs and said many prayers for their peoples. And Sparrow kept on adding more wood to the fire. This went of for a while until Coyote let negative thoughts invade his mind instead of being there for his heart.

Now we already know how Coyote's mind works? Well, he thought

Dance of the Nighthawk

Sparrow was trying to make it a competition of who would be strongest to handle the heat of the fire, when Sparrow had no such intentions. Sparrow was there for the purification and his heart. Coyote was not in his heart and became confused on what to do so he turned to his trickster ways and convinced Sparrow that it was way too hot for him, and that he couldn't handle the heat, so that Sparrow could do no harm to him, for he knew that Sparrow had strong medicine. So Sparrow obliged and opened the door for Coyote to leave for the river to cleanse himself.

Coyote proceeded immediately to devise a plan to get even with the innocent Sparrow. He would show Sparrow that he could stand the heat more than he had pretended to. So he would be the first one up in the morning and would gather the wood and get the fire ready bright and early. It was only right that they took turns, so it was his turn to show Sparrow what a warrior he was. So, the next morning when Sparrow flew up, he was amazed that Coyote had everything in order and was ready to go so early. Sparrow had some suspicions but they quickly subsided because Sparrow was there for his heart.

"Boy, you got that fire going hot and early, kinsman," Sparrow said.

Coyote replied, "I know how you liked it so hot yesterday that I didn't want to disappoint my comrade and have a mediocre fire." So they entered *Apyoke* and Coyote closed the door and started to add wood to the fire. The fire was nice and hot and even had a little roar to it. Coyote-asked Sparrow how he was doing? Bat answered that he was okay and added a few more logs to the fire. Once again Coyote asked how Sparrow was doing and the fire was getting louder he could barely hear him and thought he heard Sparrow say he was fine. But Sparrow was really having a hard time.

Once more Coyote asked Bat how he was doing and, after he didn't get a reply, Coyote thought Sparrow was pretending to be asleep and was trying to out do him. Oh boy! There goes that mind of Coyote again. So he threw on more wood. The whole time it really was getting hot and Sparrow was yelling and yelling from the back but Coyote couldn't hear him over the song of the fire. All of sudden the lodge burst into flames and Coyote just made it out by the tip of his tail… (and every time you see him, the tip of his tale looks burnt.) However, Sparrow wasn't so lucky to escape. All Coyote could do, was a wait for the fire to subside, smoke his pipe and try to remember a certain song that his uncle had taught him.

You see, one of the many powers that are included in Coyote's arsenal is that he has the power to bring back the breath into anybody. He was practicing this ritual early on in life, so he sang the song his uncle taught him and jumped over Sparrow 3 times until Bat stirred and awakened. Sparrow was

Dance of the Blackbird

stunned as he looked into those big black eyes of his best friend. He forgave Coyote on sight, without thinking, because he brought him back to life and he now knew that they were both in the heart. That is why Sparrow is so black and comes out only at night to hunt. If you are wondering if they are still comrades and go to war for the *Wot*? Oh yeah, except the rules have changed a little bit. Bat flies ahead in the darkness to find the enemies because he blends into the darkness so well and you can still hear Coyotes war song at night.

Now let's talk about ego. We all know that Coyote is a trickster. However, not many know about his big ego! Ask the four legged, flying and swimming people, they know him very well and will tell ya all about his crazy antics! This is Wookpecker's story (*Pu la kak*) and he's sticking to it.

You see, Wookpecker is one of them flyers who was gifted with a powerful beak to hide his most favorite food *Hutash* (Mother Earth) grows, acorns. He hides, and stockpiles loads of the tasty acorns in the hardness of the oak trees he gathers them from as well as having the reputation for having the most brilliant, reddest head in the territory. And Coyotes ego would sure get a big boost from that. Just think what it would feel like to be the only Coyote in the territory to have a brilliant red head, what prestige and influence that would carry? He thought about it constantly. This desire and wanting hit like the flash floods that announce the start of the rainy season. An alignment that also included Wookpecker hiding acorns in the tops of an oak tree getting ready for the upcoming winter. Hide em' up as high as you can was his belief! The closer to the Sky people, the better.

Coyote was cruising by Wookpecker's place when he saw that crimson glow of *Pu la kaks* head. It seemed to put him in a trance and he would get all light headed from the overwhelming warmth the glowing red head brought him. He had to have one! He tried not to get to close, he knew he wouldn't have any control over his actions. So he kept his distance and devised, for many months, different plans to obtain that mysterious red head.

During the time of fall, Coyote figured it would be good timing, but he had to keep his composure. From his vantage point high in the trees while hiding his acorns, *Pu la kak* could see that darn Coyote down there snooping around again and acting like the small bird couldn't see him. He knew that Coyote envied and drooled over the color of his *doo* and wondered what he was up to now? This day Coyote couldn't control himself and just got all goofy and light headed and he yelled at the top of his lungs, "Hey *Pu la kak* how did you get your head so red?" *Pu la kak* couldn't believe his red ears.

That darn Coyote is out his mind down there. He's gone plum loco! Like I'm gonna let him in on my magic and tell him my secret? So this went on for most of the day, until Coyote decided that he was going to bring all the baskets of acorns that he had won gambling and arranged them at the bottom of *Pu la kaks* tree and try to bust a deal with him.

At first, *Pu la kak* did a good job of ignoring him, but couldn't ignore those juicy, plump acorns and drooled and slobbered all over them. His mouth didn't want to stop watering, they smelled so good. He tried to stall and stall so he could get the best deal and not to give in to Coyote and reveal too much information, especially getting caught up in his mesmerizing look, that would put him in a trance and open him up for Coyote's manipulations. So as they tried to work each other, they conversed and shared small talk about how it was to fly or run. They both asked and wondered what happened to the baby fawn? Neither of them hadn't seen the lil' whippersnapper in some time.

By now, grandfather Sun was getting closer to his house in the west and he had to go and prepare all the beings he had gathered during the day for his two daughters. His daughters and he would enjoy the evening feast, rest up, and allow space for the night movements to have their time. *Pu la kak* prefers to stay tucked in his hole at this time or else he would be chased all night by all the night beings who find him a delicious meal. However, Coyote didn't let him fall asleep! Every time he dozed off, Coyote threw an acorn at him to wake him up and get his attention. He would yell, "Hey *Pu lu kak* how did you get your head so brilliantly red?" And this was slowly playing on his nerves, patience and he was growing very tired and scared of the night beings.

Finally, he blurted out in a half sincere way, " I put a hot rock on it!" That's all Coyote needed to hear "C-Ya", and he was off to his *Ap* (house) lickity split! He started to build a fire and look for a rock that would fit his head that left a good feeling in his heart. Now that was a dilemma and a half. Coyote was more in the mind than in the heart. What size? "I want the brightest, reddest, head in the whole darn territories", Coyote's ego thought.

So different size rocks and more wood went on the fire. Throughout the night, Coyote and his battle went back and forth to create a fire hot enough and to find a rock the right size for his new bright red head. Meanwhile, *Pu la kak* was snuggled-up and warm, dreaming of where he was going to hide all those delicious acorns! Now Coyote is one of them persistent fellahs, "Another all nighter," he mused? He was going to be up all night again with one of his kooky schemes! Classic Coyote. So he put more wood on the fire. How was he going pick up all those hot rocks? And he wasn't going to just put one on! He was pilling dem' on, just like in the sweat lodge! He was gonna need to make some forked sticks and other utensils. He was in his mind again and it was going a mile a minute and then he suddenly thought, "What a dummie I've been? The answer is blazing right in front of me!" So he stuck his head right into the fire!

So listen very carefully during and between the twilight and the dawn, open yourself up and you could hear him yelling and yipping, "Owwwwooohhhhoooo!" Up to one of his kooky schemes. That darn *Hoo Haw.*

And Coyote knows how to spin a tail or two! Yes indeed! In certain circles he's also known as a story telling emeritus, (sort of), one of dem, eccentric, philanthropists. That's right, one of dem Jack of all trade guys and master of none. Heard him sayin' one time, "He really doesn't know everything, just a little bit about everything."

He loves to share his observations of the Chumash predecessors, especially those during the time of the Missions. Many were into public displays of power using fast witted responses to show the Spanish how smart they really were. One day this fellah finds himself given a pair of hide sandals from this padre who thought to ease the native's bare feet from any discomfort as he saw fit. The native didn't wear them, or tried them on and just draped them over his shoulder, showing off his wealth. When the Padre asked why the native man was not wearing the sandals he was given a few day's later, he replied that he had a crack in his foot and in it lived Cricket. If he was to wear the sandals it would trap Cricket and he would stop singing!

During a mild, foggy day a padre asked a native only clad in a breech cloth if he was cold? The native asked the fully robed from head toe padre if is face was cold? The padre answered, no! The native then replied with a sly grin that he was all face!

One of Coyote's favorite victims for his story tellin' shenanigans is Ol' Mr. Hawk. Coyote refers to him as the Hawk of Controversy. He admires the magic of his dancing feathers and how it has affected the perception of truth throughout his two legged winged journey. Seems every time that ol' Hawk decides to plant them two legs and dance it sorta stirs up the pot a lil bit. Most of all he loves the encounter ol' Hawk had with the White Deer who is living in the vicinity of the Powerful River Turtle People.

It all started a time ago when Ol' Hawk was traveling and sight seeing on one of his favorite byways when a Hawk cousin of his demanded his attention and ordered him to follow him. Over the knoll they went in a southerly direction to investigate another mystery. That Ol' Hawk could not believe what was transpiring right before his very eyes! There was a metal contraption that resembled what looked like a few four wheel all terrain vehicles with some odd looking, strangely dressed, two legged creatures doing what seemed like science fiction experiments on this helpless daughter of mother earth. What a sad time we are in, thought the Hawk. This poor Deer lady, what must she be going through? He was out of character for once. That jibber jabbering Ol' Hawk didn't have a darn thang to say! And that babbling Hawk never shuts up. He always had something to say to find a remedy or find a balance, however intimidating the task might be, when crisis crosses his path. And that Ol' Hawk has had some unbelievable, unique encounters. Maybe that is why Grandmother Moon refers to him as, "The fancy one whom is always exploring."

So as the saying goes, he prayed on it. Well, he also did a little investigating and found out, the family she belongs to was going through same tough times and displaying the same characteristics of this certain malady. So he prayed on it some more , and then a White Deer came into his vigil. He asked the deer what to do to help the poor innocent deer people. She told him to arrange it with the family of Badgers in that area, to construct a circle, to make offerings for the deer people's health and to dance for their vigor and love of life. The thing about it was that the Eagle and the Hawk had been going thru some time with that white deer long before that.

So, in a vision as clear as the waters that rush through the river of the Turtle people during the years of the Steelhead Trout, she told the Hawk not to worry. She came to help him and heard his prayers and introduced herself as fertility. And she journeyed from the center of the universe. A Red Deer and a Jackrabbit came along with her. And before the healing could start, the Red Deer and Jackrabbit would be revealed in a different form. Sort of inhuman two legged variety form. The Red Deer will be the one of wisdom and the Jackrabbit inheriting the power of will. These characteristics are stepping stones to knowledge and awareness as well as clarity. If you haven't figured it out by now, yes, the Deer people survived and all this happened during her third year residing near the powerful River Turtle people. One bit of astonishing validity to the Hawk's discipline can be seen in the birth of another white deer in the immediate vicinity of that sacred dance and celebration circle. Dat darn Coyote sure can tell a tall, tall tail? Sure!

Ya Hey, Tani Hey!

As the hunter and fisher hangs his gathering and hunting nets...

Ancient Chumash saying, regarding and refering to the "end of a story."

Glossary

Vocabulary is solely the Author's interpretation

24/7	Twenty-four hours a day, seven days a week.
Alalkoy	Dolphin
Alapkalawashaq	Families of *Kalawashaq*.
Alchucklash	*Chumash* doctor, member of elite society.
Alisha	Sun, *Samala Chumash*
Anchum	Shell bead money.
Ap	Chumash dwelling made of willow poles, and thatched with tule reeds and/or grass.
Apyoke	Traditional sweat lodge, used only by men.
Aqitsume	A village in the foothills of the *Samala* valley
Atishwun	Personal power, ritual paraphernalia and spirit helpers. Magic.
Atishwunits	One who possesses *Atishwun*.
Chiquiti	Barn owl
Conject	Slang for doin' some conjecturing.
Cuyamu	A village and territory near the center of the world, Mount Pino's.
Doo	American/English slang for hairdo.
Grandma Moy moy	Moon
Haku	Greetings, hello, salutations.
Heh leh	Hawk
He'lo	A village near Goleta slough.

Hoo Haw Swinuch	Coyote Dance of great mystery.
Hu ma liwo	Village around Malibu.
Hus	Grizzly bear
Hutash	Mother earth
Kakanupmawa	Sun
Kalawashaq	A village in the _Samala_ valley , home of the powerful _River Turtle People_.
Limuw	Santa Cruz Island
Luhui	Female Island _Wot_, Princess, vixen.
Mishtoyo	Rainbow
Molok	A plant used for smoking and healing.
Mooptafied	Derived from the _Chumash_ word _Moop ta my._ Ancient genetic memory.
Muhu	Great horned owl
Muwu	A village around Pt. Mugu.
Onok'ok	Lizard
Oh noy yo	Frog, toad
Onso	Steel head trout
Paha	Member of elite society, traditional practitioner, ceremonial officiator, captain and assistant to the _Wot. Heh leh._
Pina	Spanish, for pine tree.
Pox	Yucca plant, used, for cording and netting.
Props	Accolades, kudos, doin' someone proper.

Pu la kak	Acorn woodpecker
Pu lu ee	Great blue heron
Qaq	Raven
Quasil	A village around Refugio beach, Port o' call for *Samala Tomol* owners.
Samala Valley	Santa Ynez Valley
Slow	Golden Eagle
Soh'toh'nok'mu	A village in the *Samala* valley.
Stuk.	A village along the Santa Ynez river.
Syutun	A village near the foot of Stearns Wharf, Santa Barbara.
Tani Hey	My way of saying thank you.
Timolokinash	A time frame, a *Molok* era, time of the first people.
Tinluw	Villages and territory of *Chumash* people around *Tejon* Pass, I-5.
Tomol	*Chumash* seafaring wooden plank canoe.
Upop	A village around Pt. Conception.
Vigilize	Like vision is to visualize is vigil to vigilize.
Wot	Member of elite society, traditional practitioner, ceremonial officiator, chief of village, providence and territory, *Slow*.
Yerba Buena	Spanish name for native mint plant.
Yokuts	Native peoples residing in the territories of the San Joaquin Valley and Southern Sierra Nevada's.

Redstar begins work on a new artwork set.

Part III

I Knew There Was A Hole In The Sky...

Just Something To Share

A Conundrum

What is a conundrum, you ask yourself? Self, what is a conundrum? Self, suggested to me that a conundrum is. If our bodies are 90% water did we came out of the water? Birth through water? Are we not in an endless cycle of evaporation, including some very old relations? So, if we drink, cook and bathe with water are we not interacting with the unknown? Would it make sense that our original breath is water and air secondary? Was water our first breath of air? So if I say, for instance, our last breath is water, is it a more divine death? And is there a difference between fresh or salt water? That's a conundrum.

How about when we perspire, or sweat or urinate? Are we not in a cycle that has not been broken since the time of creation? Is it not true that we came out of the water? Theoretically speaking? Oh no! The big "E" word. Is this gonna stir up the pot a little? There, I would say to self, that surely is not a conundrum. I've heard of the great flood but not the great drought. So if the moon is a shell, then why does her spirit have so much power that it affects every woman born till she's at least 40? She is lifeless, is she not? So what's up with the ozone layer? If things happen in three's and mother earth has already done two universal cleansings that we know of? Would you not presume that fire was the first, with the dinosaurs? Did we not change appearance and character then? Does not water have a relationship with ice? Can I presume that we can correlate water with the Ice Age? Would the next surely be wind?

As a minor self proclaimed philosopher, I would say that would make sense because those are mother earth's three elements. Philosophically speaking, as a minor self proclaimed intellect as well, is it true that my father said I didn't know shit? Is that a conundrum? No, it's a stab at your father. Since it was beat into my head that I am a know it all. Wouldn't it make sense that I would believe that I don't know everything, just a little about everything? No, that's being sarcastic. I would say, now, do we have a conundrum here? Sorry Pop's. Love Ya! Brain fart or child hood trauma. Is getting personal a conundrum?

What's this all about 2013 of the Maya calendar? Do they know something, we don't? And what happened to the Incas? If scholars are shooting holes in the Bearing Strait theory, then is there a possible migration of Paleo Indians from the southern regions? Is it true what Steven Powers said of his observations of California Indians in northern California during and after the gold rush? And is it fair to call it excepted theory or conjecture and to be taught in the institutions and schools of academia as a positive analyses, or fair to all, student and native? Conundrum, indeed.

And what about the way Krober showed how ruthless he was refusing to acknowledge and include the Chumash as a major nation in his studies, graphs, tables and scribing of his anthropological babbling on the study of archeology through sifting through shell mounds of discarded debris, and describe it as major ethnological material that can be manipulated? Was not he feuding and competing with JP Harrington for funds? Now that's a co-nundrum, I would say, self. Well maybe? No, JP Harrington was studying the Chumash then. No, conundrum. And is there a possible connection linking Krober to Leon De Cesssac and his studies of Native Californians, his abruptly leaving the country, upon threat, back to France and does the mysterious disappearance of his writings and observations have anything to do with this? Is this a conundrum? Yes, that's a James Bond conundrum. Where does Harrington fit into all this.? Was he really an Angry God? See, a conundrum, or at the least a job for Bond, James Bond, 007. And doesn't pelican look like evolution to you? Excuse me, brain fart! I mean pterodac-tyl the flyer. Scientist say you can neither create nor destroy energy. So if the Sun is the most powerful energy source besides mother earth, (remem-ber the moon is dead), would not your energy be drawn like a magnet to it's power supply?

And how about, Don Juan? What did he mean when he said, "Even the Eagle has to Eat." Is that a conundrum self? I would say so. That is a conun-drum. If I was born in the 805 would that make me Chumash? Now that's a conundrum? And politicking in the wrong chapter. Sorry, don't hate. Conundrum Hater.

If mount Pino's is the largest peak in the territory and the ocean resided more towards a southern direction in our region. Would you not think that Paleo Chumash migrated south from the interior? And because Mt. Pino's regarded as the Chumash center of the world would you not presume that it is truly our birthing place or emergence out of the water for that area? No, that's theory? Sike, your mama rides a bike. How come da Rabbit not scared da Bear? Yep, it is truly a conundrum. Why does every California native nation insist on their birthing or creation spots?

Was there only one exploration out of the water by one being or were there many at different times of history? Sherlock, that's a conundrum. Or should I say I've put my size 10 into my mouth. However, I am typing. That's a conundrum. So if Moon and Sun have this thing going on wouldn't you say that he inseminates her water magic to birth rainbows. Are rainbows visions of birthing places? So could that not mean the rainbow bridge might have possibly had a connection with Mt. Pinos? After all, the milky way is the path of the ancient ones, the pine nut gatherers. Boy, are we on a conundrum. Were the first explorers out of water, breeding? Sheesh, another conundrum? Are not there beings on every millimeter of mother earth? Are not the smallest the strongest? Shall the meek truly inherit the earth?

Just something to share

Let's talk about people of prayer.

They say you gotta put it out there to be heard, right? Yes indeed. Ask and you shall receive. Seek and you shall find. So what's up with people ridiculing the man walking down the street mumbling to himself? He sure is putting it out there, is he not? Who is he talking to? He could be talking to the man himself, or even be the man? Who knows? He must be someone of strong faith if he is not embarrassed to pray in public. Just because one looks unkept and homeless does not mean that they are loony'toons or bonkers. Most of those in need are the ones on the street. So why must one assume that the downtrodden do not pray?

I know I am not ashamed of being a man of prayer and putting it out there wherever and whatever I am doing when I am in need of divine intervention, or to keep things going smooth.

Prayer comes in different forms. Singing and dancing can be considered forms of prayer. During one of my prayer sessions, it was shared with me that there is no color or prejudice where the Sky People call home, and that it goes on forever. Matter of fact, is it not replicating? The heavens above have been described as going on forever. So no one really owns it, it is truly the realm of the spirits. There is plenty of room for everybody and there is no reason to fight over it. It is a mystery in the first place. No doubt that you can argue that every soul is there, including the dinosaurs and cave men. By the way, talking about cave men, don't us Chumash people resemble the cave men? Believe it or not, we do. A majority of people really do not know about the culture or ways of California Natives. They are mainly familiar with the Native Americans of the Plains or Southwest, not to mention the classic Hollywood Indian whom have um heep um greenbacks or frog skins. We are known by those magnificent cave paintings and not to mention the bones that we wear in our hair, noses and ears. We are also well known for our use of stone, bone and wood for culinary, medicinal and daily living purposes as well as our variety of uses of the variety of skins this territory has to offer.

How about the people walking around or twitching and grabbing at images that we cannot see? What are they seeing? How come we cannot see what they do? Maybe it is the other way around. They are the fortunate ones that can see or participate in the dimension that is the realm of the departed. How about the ones that have seizures and strokes. Where do they go and see?

At this point, one must ask one's self if the secret language of the so called retarded and autistic is in reality a holy communication. Shouldn't we be taking better care of them? I've often heard, and even from some of my peoples, that those are the special ones. Back in the days before genocide and dis-ease hit these shores, those with schizophrenia and/or bipolar were revered by Native nations because you really do not know who they are talking or interacting with.

How about when spirit talks to you, or you have an encounter with a being with four legs, fur or wings, and you share that with another individual and they give you that look? You know that look? The one that implicates you as off your rocker, insane or deranged, when you definitely know that it was not your imagination! You know what you saw or heard. The eyes, ears and nose do not lie, just the mouth. That is why we have two ears, two eyes, two nostrils and just one mouth. Ask Razzle Dazzle.

So what I am really trying to say and get at is, if you slow down enough, even the most shallow nonbeliever can hear a Fairy or Elf tip toeing across their lawn or back yard. Besides, we all know, that Fairies and Elves would rather be outside with their toes in Mother Earth than being inside watching television, eating or taking a nap.

Just something to share!

Values of Knowledge Concerning Commerce

Values of knowledge concerning commerce that can contribute to your spiritual well being as well as understanding your discipline, and how it fuels your integrity to live in the times that we find ourselves in. Whether it has to do with our personal, family, working or social living situations, we need some kind of values that can fit metaphorically into our personal, spiritual and social life. There are many comparatives out there that are time tested and work.

For example:

What works for one person does not necessarily mean that it will work for another. And is it really working in the first place? And by who's standards? That is why doing your personal inventory consistently is so important in life. Better to see your unpleasant character defects and work on them yourself, than to have someone point them out to you.

I myself have consistently followed three words to help me complete this book. Through the smooth times when I did not need to depend on them as much as the hard times when I needed them the most. Just dealing with everyday life can drag the strongest down to the rock bottom, that we all hear about. It is a hard road and no one says it is going to be easy. If it was easy? Every one would be peaceful. Even the non conceivable perfect person, if there is such a being?

Three words:
- *Patience*
- *Understanding*
- *Fortitude*

Those words encompassed everything I need to aid me in the problems that I have and will encounter. What I have received from being diligent, money cannot buy. I have learned how to deeply love and respect myself instead of hurting myself as well as my family and friends.

The White Deer shares that there are three requirements to understand and interact with our traditional and spiritual beliefs of our predecessors and to how to conjure up the same aura, essence and energy field.

Three words:
- *Fertility,* to continually nurture our growth.
- *Will,* to do what it takes.
- *Wisdom,* knowing what and what not to do.

The prosperous times that us California Natives are experiencing can be seen as proof that something is working. Not to mention the times of healing we are experiencing, as well as the increased interest and reaffirmation in our culture and tradition.

These values of knowledge are just the tip of the ice berg and there is so much intertwined within each of these values that the benefits go on and on. I must stress that this is just my interpretation of this well known philosophy among most of us male Dancers. There is so much out there and this works for me. I am just suggesting this as a tool to use in life. I am not an expert, nor a college graduate. Most of this is common sense. However, what is common sense for one, can be so hard for another to understand if they did not have the privilege to grow up in a loving family home, sans the dysfunctions.

Responsibility, to family and friends.
Compensation, whether it is love or money.
Limitation, whether it is greed or being frugal.
Moderation, not overdoing it as well as completing what you started.
Restitution includes, Karma, fate and accountability.

It sounds so simple, does it not?
Maybe that it is why they say to keep it simple?

So the most likely suggestion to life is not to make it so complicated that you cannot face any situation that detours your well-being and peace of living in this turbulent world.

Just something, I wanted to share.

Just Something To Share
Chumash Politicking

This might seem a little eccentric, out of the ordinary, off kilter or not follow the protocol of normal literary work, however, when you get a shot, take a shot and nock it into another dimension and set a precedent. This is an editorial that I never submitted for review by the editor and editorial staff of the Santa Barbara News-Press for consideration to be published, to address statements made in the Santa Barbara News-Press by a few people of the Chumash Nation.

In August of 2002 a Chumash male youth snuck his way onto the Santa Barbara Mission stage, uninvited, during a performance by representative of the Santa Ynez *Chumash* Indian Reservation and made verbal attacks and showed violent intentions towards the dancers, including a 9-year-old girl from the reservation. The event was to celebrate the Old Spanish Days of Santa Barbara. This had been the second year in a row the Chumash Reservation was invited to the celebration and have dancers represent them.

Being invited was a milestone in Chumash history and we have every right to be proud and show the community at large how respectful we carry ourselves these days and even fund an event that has a festering wound that still has affects on our community today. We were able to freely express ourselves and participate in a movement of our culture with pure hearts without the scrutiny of the padres and/or Spanish soldiers in that proximity and fanfare being recorded and televised by a local station. It hasn't been that long since our predecessors and families toiled and lost their lives to build the Missions of California. Next to the Mission steps is the cemetery. Some and most of our relations of the Chumash Nation are buried there including a very special Lady Islander. I was personally was there for them, their spirit and my belief in healing.

Those dances were and are about positive energy! I understand the hatred and have the same dis-easement of prejudice. However, it's a negative energy that I'm learning to avoid, so let's just call this a lil' backslide. This letter was never submitted because at the time I felt that I would just be feeding into a bunch of negative energy that was being shown to the general public who wasn't privy to the whole picture or knew the sincerity of the dancers and their supporters. I felt like I was being sucked into a no holds bar, sleeves rolled up, old time fisticuffs or as the Joker would say, "old dooker roo", in the public forum! I could sling mud myself, ol' boy here, got's some smut he could toss around like a Cesar salad. However, I refused to lower myself to that level and exercised a level more appropriate to my timing, integrity and culturing. So I gave it to the spirits to take care of and have faith that an opportunity for myself would arise. So the decision to actually have the audacity to print this letter in this forum should be of no surprise to the people who know me and my intense spontaneity to conform to my determination and reputation in Chumash territory. I'm told my reputation precedes me? So I am getting on with doing this on my terms with even more tackiness and/or tack that was portrayed in a very embarrassing thugish way, to the people of this territory. This here is tacky, Oooowwwwooooohhhh!"

Some of the comments here may not make sense to the ordinary person, who has no idea of what I'm writing about, however to all others of concern, you need not any help to decipher what I have scribed here. As far as where we are at today? That Chumash youth was just expressing in his way that he wanted in. So he made his presence known. Now he's on a better path. Funny how things work out? Special attention to the teachers: please do not read this to the lil' tikes and school children... or do that grammar check thing.

To: Editor and staff, Santa Barbara News Press
From: David Paul Dominguez

In regards to the assault on the dancers representing the Santa Ynez Reservation on the Mission steps during the Old Spanish Days La Fiesta Pequena celebration of 2002.

I would like to voice my opinion and wisdom as the Chumash traditional male dancer who was dancing and participating that evening. During my path and journey as a traditional dancer, intertribal pow-wow dancer and practitioner of Chumash tradition. It has been my perspective that anytime any people congregate to celebrate and/or worship it is a sacred event. They are universal and have been practiced since the dawn of time and more than likely, are intertwined with belief systems and struggles. Fiesta gained its momentum from a Chumash ritual observance or movement. That alone should be respected and taken into one's perspective, motivation and intentions. Today in this time frame that we find ourselves in, we have different spiritual and social class struggles in Chumash territory. This here primitive incident aligns itself in the category of a spiritual struggle and is in a class of it's own and owes up to a very different dynamic and energy that takes years to recognize and discipline yourself to be one with.

No matter if small or large spiritual struggles should be respected as all struggles are. Spiritual victory contributes to personal enlightenment and state of conscientiousness for spiritual survival. They contribute to our people's tradition, culture, understanding, awareness and cohesiveness as tribal people. Tribal traditional people of higher awareness and conscientiousness know that it is a spiritual struggle to dance. It's not just dance. It's an expression of enlightenment and a way to communicate with ones heart with the spirit world. Most of the Chumash people who have spoken out for or against our participation have the birthright or earned the respect in the native community to say what they feel.

Only the spirits have the right to judge our prayers or practice. It seems though that there are still a few Chumash people out there in Chumash territory who are not open enough to know that divided we fall. The Native and new people have a saying about too many Chiefs and not enough Indians. I would like to remind the minority of native people of this precious territory of ours, if you are or are not participating in any of the ritual observances, pow-wows, gatherings, social functions or any of the movements that make Chumash territory harmonious and powerful as it still is, be courteous and kind.

Keep your opinions to yourself or step up to the plate like many of us, who are respecting and honoring the spirits and families of our past with the same resourcefulness and vigor. Many of us are making head ways and contributions in arenas such as politics, Indian gaming, Tribal Councils, Tribal programs, environmental and land issues, cultural resources, medical, education, spiritual and traditional preservation. That's where the front lines are at in these times. We need not to pursue activism, We are in different times and are no longer considered a lower class nor do we need to act like one. It's not the 60's or 70's anymore. Ot'2 baby! Us dancers danced with all our hearts with spirits watching, guiding and protecting us and in no way did any of us dishonor our predecessors who lost their lives to the battle of genocide at the hands of the invaders. We were dancing and participating to show our respect when we were rudely interrupted by an angry youth with no direction. Shame on you! Angry youth with no direction! If you hate Fiesta and the Spanish so much, why didn't you celebrate and bring the attention to Chumash territory of the atrocities our families suffered? Oh wait! You did that! And most of the new people know that our families suffered! So what do you do now? Us Chumash people are here today because of the blood, sweat, and tears that built the beautiful reminders of Chumash craftsmanship and endurance referred to as missions.

I have never been enslaved, have you? Thanks for participate in the battle. It was the right place but wrong time. At least you made us all fully aware of your integrity and your angry youth with no direction.

We need that kind of "that a boy's or girl's " like we need the atrocities and dis-ease that went on. The native and new people have another saying about not judging an Indian till you walk a mile in his or her moccasins. Have a little respect for us Chumash people and our endeavors. As native people we have to practice to keep our traditions alive. I suggest, to the angry youth with no direction, to practice a reputation as a peer and not a thug. People will listen to you instead of tackling you and hauling you off to jail.

You are in a unique position with some momentum. I would suggest that you take advantage of it and attempt or accomplish some progress out of the unbalance and/or balance you have gifted us Chumash people with. As for as social class struggles go, that's another lesson and another time and venue. I'm not the bad guy. I'm just throwing soft rocks and hard truth. Not to break out the salt or add insult to injury, however, the Intertribal Drum we were dancing to wasn't Apache. With all do respects to the Apache Nation. Duh! Is this 200 and 50 words or less?

Respectively,
David Paul Dominguez
Tokya. Chumash Cultural Arts

Just Something to Share
Reading the riot act.

As tribal peoples, we were and are burdens for spiritual punishment. Nowadays, we are also burdens for physical punishment. Let me try to explain this as simply as I can. When an individual, family, or clan would encounter a roadblock in their lives, they would seek out the remedy from the peoples who were responsible for keeping the balance with the spirit world.

The ones who were experiencing a relationship, through ritual, with the spirit world. More than likely, those persons would put themselves through extra, out of the ordinary, feats of physical endurance to open a portal or portals to make contact through various states of consciousness. They would act as conduits for the spirits to guide and influence the aiding to remedy the situation, whether small or large, without hesitation and/or prejudice. Respecting and recognizing the power of healing, they would recommend their kinsmen to follow suit and do the same with commitment, consistency and sincerity. This might involve fasting, sleep deprivation, sitting, standing in one place for a multitude of hours, singing power songs, and complimenting them with the graceful movements of the body.

Ceremony, ritual or solar observances, are also involved. We were burdens for spiritual punishment. Every movement or moment has an opposite or a negative effect to it. In this case, we are now burdens for physical punishment. Nowadays, we turn to addictions, treating our bodies as waste sites. We abuse our spouses and children, while setting poor examples of parenthood, manhood, as well as womanhood.

You cannot blame a youngster for doing what he did if he wasn't taught correctly, or didn't know any better.

Right? Or Wrong?

Egos and self-indulgence make us insensitive to our fellow beings and selfishness reigns instead of selflessness. The herd have turned into beings of comfort, materialism, and wasting time on frivolities. Who are we to be exempt from the rigors of life that our family lineages have known for thousands of years, which is solely responsible for keeping our societies in balance without invasion from the frivolities, embellishments and materialism that lure and steal us away from our tribal responsibility and our true roots of whom we really are? Poor, Pitiful, Two-Leggeds. We humans are very old and ancient, sacred beings—a life force thousands of years old.

I tell all the people that approach me and say that they feel the Indian in them, and that somewhere down their bloodline it has to be there. But we are all tribal peoples first, and have the same humble beginnings. We all come from the caves working the stone and bone. Universally we are all basically the same. So why do people have to hate and force their opinion, lifestyle, or loneliness on another? Be the example! Set the standard instead of trying to fit into something that doesn't work for you. It all starts with culture and tradition. Hilary is right you know. It *does* take a village to raise a child. Us tribal people are used of being raised with all our kin around us. From Grandparents to Aunts, Uncles and Cousins, we were used to really being a family culture. Nowadays, it's everyone for themselves.

My heart really goes out to the young men out there who have to face manhood head on at 18. It usually goes like this: first, you are raised by your mother because your father was either a drunk, drug addict or spouse abuser. Second, you are an adult and you can stay out all night. So now your mom is bitching at you to either get a job or go to school because, according to what society has taught her, that's what it takes to be a man? That's just a shallow human being, following the herd! So now you're stuck in this endless shit hole that consumes your every core of having been bred for thousands of years to be a leader, or part of a powerful, intellectual, providing group of leading men that were responsible for many lives in their tribe or clan. Not only that, you are also caught in another endless, depressing, low self-esteem, no prospect life that starts around noon or so, sleeping off the fogginess that stole your night of star gazing and communing with the spirits that rule the night. Yep, that is the stone cold truth how we Native men are to fit in or conform to a society of men that constantly floats at the bottom of the muck.

There are no more gentlemen's agreements; no brotherhood. It's a dog eat dog world out there with all the backstabbing, horns-waggling, flim-flaming, and land grabbing. Do as I say, not as I do? Shouldn't it be the rule of acceptance to live the advice you are giving, for it is affecting a human being whom trusts your advice for life. Remember, we are here for just a short time—Pebbles in the sand! Most importantly, remember we are in the spirit world for so long.

David Paul Dominguez

Printed in the United States
222208BV00005B/2/P

9 780971 317031